A PASSING WEST

ALSO BY DAGOBERTO GILB

a passing

west

ESSAYS FROM THE BORDERLANDS

Dagoberto Gilb

ILLUSTRATIONS BY César A. Martínez

HIGH ROAD BOOKS
ALBUQUERQUE

Printed in the United States of America

First Paperback Edition, 2025

ISBN 978-0-8263-6682-5 (cloth)
ISBN 870-0-8263-6890-4 (paper)
ISBN 978-0-8263-6683-2 (ePub)

Library of Congress Control Number: 2024940512

Founded in 1889, the University of New
Mexico sits on the traditional homelands of the
Pueblo of Sandia. The original peoples of New
Mexico—Pueblo, Navajo, and Apache—since time
immemorial have deep connections to the land
and have made significant contributions to the
broader community statewide. We honor the land
itself and those who remain stewards of this land
throughout the generations and also acknowledge
our committed relationship to Indigenous peoples.
We gratefully recognize our history.

Cover illustration: Adapted from photos by Brandon
Frie and Diego DH on Unsplash

Designed by Isaac Morris

Interior line art by César A. Martínez

Composed in Adobe Caslon, Concave Tuscan, and
Rosewood.

PRAISE FOR *A PASSING WEST*

"The charm of Dagoberto Gilb's *A Passing West* is apparent quickly—in the wit, the granular observations, and the distinctive, rollicking style of his prose—but that charm can be deceptive. The scope and gravity of this collection gather force over time.

"*A Passing West* is rooted in Chicano California, Texas, and the greater Southwest, but it journeys far beyond—back and forth across the US-Mexico border, to the cornfields of Iowa, the deep South, and a vast archive of the Spanish conquest of Mesoamerica in Sevilla. It stops in restaurants, garages, and construction sites along the way.

"In these dispatches and meditations, Gilb proves himself a journeyman—a self-made Mexican American author from the working class, immersed in and inspired by books. He celebrates the dignity and durability of both intellectual and manual labor and the people who do it.

"Gilb's voice is funny, contentious, absurd, and learned. The essays challenge, entertain, and illuminate. Taken together they amount to a unique chronicle of a culture and people, both migratory and deeply rooted, whose immense presence and contributions to the fabric of American life have been historically diminished, obscured, and purposefully hidden. *A Passing West* marks an important contribution to the art of the essay and a distinguished achievement in this author's fifty-year career. We are honored to select it for this year's award."—*From the PEN America Judges' Citation for the Diamonstein-Spielvogel Award*

"Like someone scoring a tree trunk with a knife to leave a mark of their passage, Dagoberto Gilb's work marks a presence on behalf of Chicanos, whose complex identity he reflects with such familiarity that he takes it for granted. It's not a question of explaining anything. His is a visceral response, a bang on the table: 'We don't matter. For them, Chicano culture doesn't exist. We are a collection of tropes, stereotypes, and clichés. We don't think about ourselves following their rules, because their rules have us all as immigrants.'"—Nicolás Dale Leal, *El País*

"The whole Southwest is his stage. He revisits childhood, marriage, literary snobbery, and Mexican history with rough care. Gilb's trouble is authentic and the stuff of literary craftsmanship. No one writes like him."—Gary Soto, author of *A Simple Plan*

"One of the most powerful writers in his generation."—Larry McMurtry

"Dagoberto Gilb is a national treasure. In these essays we ride with him on his mad journey—from high-rise construction worker to pioneering man of letters to unstoppable Latino literary force of nature."—Héctor Tobar, author of *Our Migrant Souls*

"Dagoberto Gilb's *A Passing West* is a potent and incisive addition to American letters. His essays tackle matters such as racism, city life, education, the politics and history of Latinx publishing and writing, and the relationship between work and citizenship. His writings are both thought-provoking and passionate. Excellent!"—Yxta Maya Murray, author of *The Queen Jade* and *God Went Like That*

"One of the most important American writers of his generation, Dagoberto Gilb has created exquisite works of fiction that have cast the Chicano experience as the site of the universal. In this collection of his nonfiction, Gilb displays that same mastery of prose, meditating on family, work, art, love, identity, and the very stuff that makes the human condition both confounding and exalting."—Oscar Villalon, editor of *ZYZZYVA*

"Un trip fantástico through the reading and the life of a celebrated Chicano writer: devastating in its honesty, stunning in its knowledge."—Santiago Vaquera-Vasquez, author of *One Day I'll Tell You the Things I've Seen: Stories*

"His meditations on Mexican American identity and life in the West take readers to dusty El Paso highways and on harrowing El Camino rides. We visit an industrial laundry facility in Los Angeles, elegant archivos in Spain, and cornfields in Iowa. In one essay, Gilb contends with overzealous border patrols on both sides of the international boundary; in another, he humorously describes the Texas origins of Sheryl Crow's first hit. Through vivid prose and poignant observation, the PEN Award winner situates Chicano history, culture, and lived experiences at the heart of the borderlands and beyond."—*New Mexico Magazine*

En memoria de mi carnal
Danny Ochoa, QEPD
        and for
Bill T, seer
Claude, union brother
Beth, more than an editor
        and
Annie, the Nobel path
        and familia
Rebeca,
Antonio Carlos,
Ricardo Angel

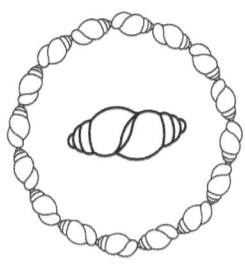

CONTENTS

II

III

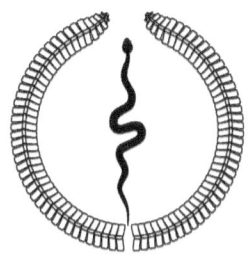

PREFACE

Though I spent almost two adult decades as a carpenter and construction worker, I am a writer of fiction. Sadly for me, especially of short fiction. Publishers, who are business people not philanthropists, want stories like they want poetry. No, they want money. They want movie rights. They want writers to be marketing celebrities who wish to be inspirational who can be as good as TV and radio personalities and truly love social media. Me, I want my work to get attention, not me. Stories, short like they are, aren't big, don't holler, don't go big screen like *Titanic* or *Gone with the Wind*. Stories are to novels as Chuang-tzu is to Kant. Much as I love the prose of García Márquez, Rulfo's stories never leave me.

Do you really imagine they want a book of essays very much? And about Chicanos? Major publishers, and by that I mean the center of American literature, on the East Coast, in New York, were very not interested. There was never a doubt. And so I am truly happy to come home again. Thank you to the University of New Mexico Press, my neighborhood book publisher and neighbors and friends (gracias muchísimas, Elizabeth Hadas), who, in 1993 under similar circumstances with my first book, *The Magic of Blood*, published what was rejected by, no exaggeration, every major editor and publisher. UNM Press *wanted* this book of essays too.

Nonfiction, these essays are another version of my want to write prose with the constraint and discipline of poetry. To capture, to have been alert to images over ideas. That haunt and linger, slow down, alter perspective. Not to plot and advance political points but to reach the art source of the brain, not the momentary rhetorical, political blah. The method: Small scenes over catchy endings, tight sentences and graphs over lots of pages.

These essays are not ordered by date of publication. Publication time often lags or jumps the timing of thoughts. The sequencing here follows my own intuition only. All the pieces are since the publication of my earlier collection of essays, *Gritos*.

I do in fact have a large advocacy that I am trying to project in this collage of pieces: There is a Mexican America, and it has been and still is growing in the Southwest region of the United States, what first was claimed, its mountains and rivers named, by Spain, what was Mexican land until the Treaty of Guadalupe Hidalgo. That the rest of the country wants to not know, or not care, or not respect its long history, aware of its architecture and cuisine but not its people, is the subject of much of this book.

—Dagoberto Gilb
Colonia Coyoacán
Mexico City, 2023

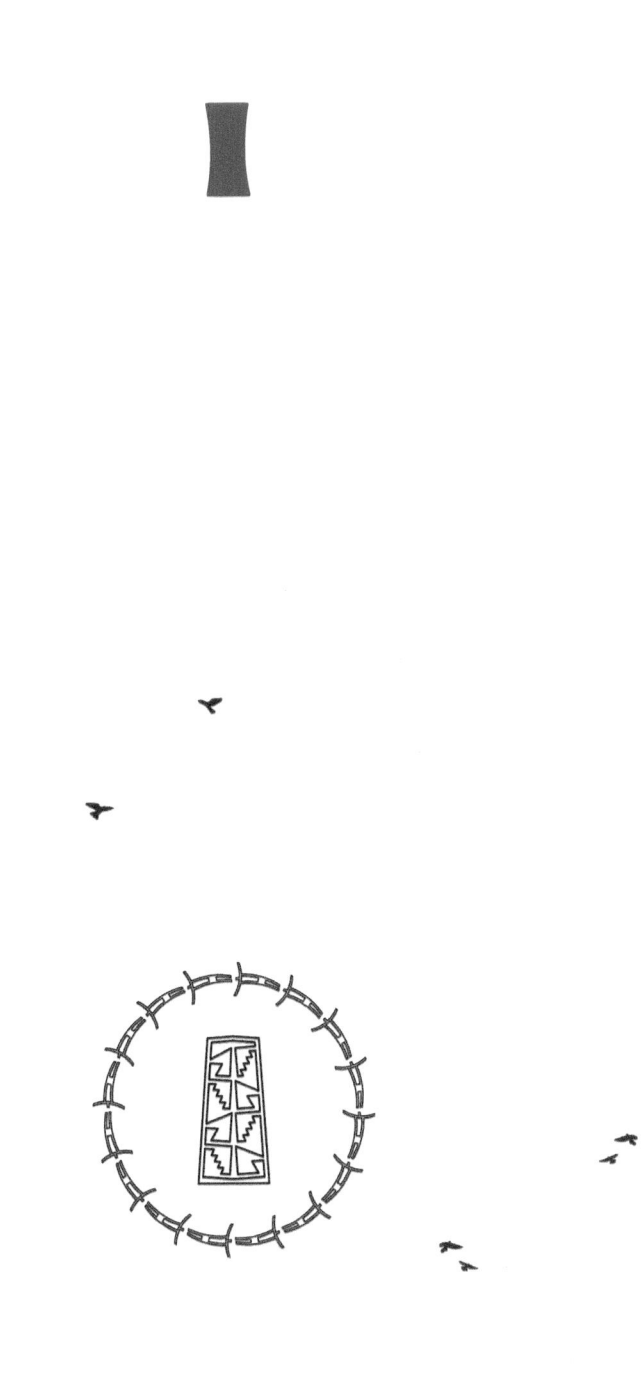

A PASSING WEST

I don't know what El Paso del Norte—mostly what we know as Ciudad Juárez—was called way before the Spaniards were on the scene naming all, but the Indigenous people saw El Paso as a north-south point of passage. At the time of the Pueblo Revolt, which led many Indigenas to create new settlements beside the Río Bravo, it was still seen as central to a north-south route. It wasn't until the massive migration of American settlers that the focus redirected the region as going from east to west. The Mexican town, what was on the northern side of the renamed Río Grande, became the American city not part of Juárez but on the other side, an east-west oriented border city dominated by a railroad business and compass. That era is receding, and El Paso has again, 500 plus years later, become a major north-south port of entry and egress for the passage of products, culture, and people.

A THOUSAND YEARS AGO, I was half of a young couple, attractive if I may be allowed, the happy parents of two handsome children, the big one still willing to hold the hand of his beautiful mom, the baby still in a four-wheel collapsible that was more a rolling hammock. We didn't have much. A lousy "good" car, income to pay the monthly rent eleven months a year, our home with barely enough furnishings to look lived in. I knew a few who weren't better off, but also a few who were, who made car payments, found steady employment that could turn out to be career choices, newer clothes and cooler shoes. Did we have "ideals" that locked us down? That explained why we were staying too poor and not running from poor El Paso, where we wanted to live? No, that's not what I said then or would now. True, I didn't want my wife to work because we had two small children who needed to be with their mom while they were so young. No ideals in my simple mind. Aside from less favorable alternatives, it seemed naturally connected to the pregnancies themselves. False, that we had lots of better options. We'd recently moved back to El Paso from years in Los Angeles, until, finally, we were happy.

One very fine day in the '80s, we were either coming from or going to the McDonald Observatory, or the fort in Fort Davis, or Marfa's lights, or Big Bend—any of those places was possible, the purpose or timing vague after these thousand years. What is a stuttered, Super-8-like memory was that we were standing at what must have been a highway pullover, staring over at El Capitan and the Guadalupe Mountains. Like most, I loved a blue sky that was from the feet up, from this end and corner to that. But it was better still with the howling, hard blow of the West Texas wind, bending the creosote and sage. Higher than any in Texas, the mountain peak is not all that big to anyone who's seen the many bigger. But they're not in the Chihuahuan Desert, and El Capitan is, a limestone tomb carved craggy like an old Mescalero's face.

We were not alone, though I don't know if we got there before or after. All I remember is a young blonde woman who, with distant years and evidence aside, I assumed was accompanied. She was wide-eyed, cheery, curious. My wife and I liked her for this, hard to not. Traveling across the American West, she was from Holland or Denmark or Sweden or Germany. In other words, she spoke English precisely, as though each syllable came from a distinct thought. There were many back and forths between us, none of which I remember whatsoever, except: Where we were from, standing in the ancient desert, the history of the Southwest as visible as an agave's thorn, meant descent—my wife Mexican, me Mexican and German—but where we lived, my wife told her, was El Paso.

She responded quickly. "El Paso? Isn't that the armpit of Texas?" She enunciated each syllable innocently, no building sarcasm or contempt, to a sincere question mark, as though quizzically recalling a geographic phrase she'd read in a paperback travel guide. It was as if she'd learned that New Mexico's slogan was "Land of Enchantment," while this armpit one was what went on El Paso's license plates.

I have no memory after that moment. As happy as we were out in the wind, in the sun, under blue sky, we were as happy in our quarry rock home, every night black and starry gorgeous outside it, nothing but quiet. We were happy inside together, all together, all better. We loved El Paso. How did bright people like us—both of us educated exceptions to family histories—find this place so beautiful to live? Why do people not from El Paso find it so ugly?

• • •

With John Wesley Harding buried on boot hill and Pancho Villa its most legendary resident, an untamed West is El Paso's lure for visiting outsiders who see history not as the past alone. They're pulled all in by the mythic (which is to say, not the visible) charms of the winding Río Grande and dangerous border. Hot red chile enchiladas still digesting, they're remembering a horse they once rode, or dreaming of the one they could've or should've—and done that and not just this. They are at a spacious, sparkly downtown bar, a double whiskey no ice, or a shot of tequila. And if there were a shake of love? Yes, it's a song coming!

Out in the West Texas town of El Paso
I fell in love with
a Mexican girl
Nighttime would find me
in Rosa's Cantina
Music would play and Felina would whirl.

The lyrics of the 1959 hit "El Paso" by Marty Robbins have fixed a romanticized country-western fantasy onto the city for over sixty-five years. It is not one that nests inside native residents of the city—read, the 90-plus percent Mexican American population of a million—but what has become an awareness of the other culture that views theirs as exotic.

Consider, if you will, the possibility of a hit song about a hot, wicked, evil, blue-eyed "dancer" named Jane in an all-Anglo club on the dimly lit perimeter of a city. Two Mexicans fight over her attentions (she was sharing a drink with the more handsome, younger new guy), one kills the other, and he flees through the back door, peeling out for the safe badlands. But the *vato*, the dude, can't bear to exist without his Jane's love. So he goes back where he's not too welcome.

They're waiting for him. A windstorm of bullets at him, but not until a blast hits his chest does he quit moving forward. Now Jane rushes out of the club and, as he is dying, kneels by him, kissing his cheek, cradling him. He kisses sweet Jane goodbye.

Though more what you'd imagine seeing on an episode of *Cops*, the tale is recounted as a nostalgic romance—of the bad, dark woman, of the manly cowboy, crossing borders, living fearlessly—for those whose Jane is Felina.* It's hard to deny that it's not the best image for El Paso's women to start out from, as opposed to, say, a French woman's, even one from LA, and so on. Doubtful it's the model El Paso would choose either. Though not everybody, for example, thinks of the JFK assassination as Dallas, it lingers steadily, a second if not first thought. Chicago hasn't seen Al Capone since the '30s, yet when people go mentally or even really, it's him. These are what

---

* I wondered about the unusual name. Though in a follow-up song by Robbins, Felina became Feleena (which to me looks Arabic), I asked friends if they ever knew any woman named Felina, the dancer in the original hit. Only professor and writer Rolando Hinojosa replied yes. It was during the Feria del Libro in Guadalajara, and part of a dinner conversation about strange Mexican customs. This Felina was a young man, not necessarily a transvestite, who wore women's clothing, which is not only tolerated but is an old tradition in Oaxaca. After this bit of research, the song and the entire bar situation took on a whole new dynamic for me.

tourists are drawn in by, and El Paso takes what it's given, as any city would. And it's not to say that everybody, everywhere doesn't want to fall in love with the outlaw, or the sexiest, or be free of civilized restrictions other than those defined by Freud and guns, living life as an adventure. El Paso as the last outpost of the Old West isn't a bad business.

• • •

It's the border town in this adventure fantasy that's kind of the problem. Because the border is "foreign," while El Paso is not in a foreign country, and it's not supposed to be treated as though it were. It just is. Not Bulgaria, Laos, Uruguay, or Canada. Mexico. Maybe not one for one exactly. Maybe only almost, somewhat. Whatever proportion, it's more than enough. Ask Texans what they think of when they think of El Paso, and there's no doubt if not specifically Juárez (more so now, way wrongly, than ever because of the narco violence), it's generally Mexico. That's not to say that there aren't positives about having an association with our culturally rich, beautiful friend with a shared past in this state and our country. There's the tradition of fine art and architecture, the historical missions and trails. There are the ornately staged and costumed folklorico dances, mariachis with brass, strings, and famed boleros and corridos, musica ranchera and American tejano. Above all, there are the plates of tacos and enchiladas, the flour tortilla, fajitas: All of this is extraordinarily popular within and across ethnic lines. And it's now all become a source of pride in Texas, but even more *as* Texas.

Unfortunately, the city that has benefited here is San Antonio, not El Paso. That's because San Antonio is not a border town. Far from Mexico, it's seen as a safe American city with a huge tourist center that especially highlights all of the above, lucratively, on its River Walk.

El Paso shares the border with Juárez. To those driving through on I-10, a subliminally dangerous Mexico, a kind of cheap motels scary. If the River Walk is perceived as what's best about Mexico, El Paso gets too much of what's not. And the worst of it is the stereotypes that reach back a century or more.

Is it only coincidence that the ugliest things that outsiders say about the city and its residents are the same about Mexicans in neighborhoods everywhere? We have all heard them in their formal disguises and convoluted euphemisms. It really comes down to poverty. In this country's history, I suppose dislike of Mexican poverty only looks a lot like racism. A couple of the dumbest canards are that these are people who don't care about speaking English (and, oddly, don't speak Spanish properly either) or that the girls get pregnant so young because it's Mexican in nature. The same nature keeps their abilities, their jobs, menial and low-paying, the same heritage doesn't believe in the value of educating its children. And . . . look at the dirty streets.

Can't be that many who are so naïve as to confuse issues of poverty, a socioeconomic condition, with the essence of a people. Or a city they live in. But I ask you right now to recall that European visitor outside the city limits who simply acquired her information impersonally.

This lowly projection is not just offensive and a few levels of wrong; it's plain off about El Paso—factually untrue, false, particularly there, where a population of strong, good families reaches back to the Mexican and American eras. Texas is not Arizona, and not like it either, where a list of Mexican character flaws would be longer and racist in all ways public but that one word. In Texas, even the worst bigots are polite and believe that it's better to say nothing if you don't got nothing decent to say. El Paso doesn't have the economies of Houston or Dallas or Austin. It is poor. And poor doesn't look as bright lights, fashion glamorous, haute cuisine, big stadium, or high-tech as rich.

· · ·

If not outright dismissed, El Paso more often feels ignored. And so it is, in the silence, six hundred miles from the state capital. Here's how I've heard it explained: She is the dark child of a crazy night on the border, and married Austin pays his legally obliged child support. The rest of Texas ought to have sympathy for El Paso's larger, unseemly reputation. Much of the country still reports that it's what all the state, end to end, looks like for hours and hours of highway—and as unexplainably wild as the West Texas wind, even as most days are as wide blue and bright sunny as . . . most days really.

Those dirty streets of El Paso. Dry dirt that dusts up in the wind—it's absolutely true that, like on a worn horse trail, it's not held down by well-groomed, watered green meadows. In the desert, brown is the dominant earth tone. Just like in an old western. Like the Old West, one in a popular country-western song even.

There are good reasons why so many love the West—the historical fable of it, its natural beauty, the opportunity to begin it has always symbolized. Only one city is both still so landlocked in both an American past and a Mexican one, a combination that is going to be the New West: The raw forces of desert still a daily part of El Paso life, from vinegarroons and scorpions, tumbleweed and ocotillo, to the throbbing of the sun and the horizontal speed of the wind, resources of metaphor and energy. An untrampled landscape that reaches up into the Franklin Mountains and over to Hueco Tanks. A legacy of Spanish conquistadores, from canals to routes, a Native American nation transplanted after a loss in a world war–like seventeenth-century battle of cultures (the Pueblo Revolt), a settlement that has lived through the shift as the midpoint between a south-to-north national power and an east-to-west one.

We all know the one about that thin line between love and hate. Or the other one that has ignorance as bliss. I still don't remember where me and my wife and sons had been that particular day way back, staring up at El Capitan. Let's just say it was Fort Davis, a cavalry garrison erected to protect White settlers from hostile Indians. What I recall well, there and then, was how doomed those hated Apaches were. Sure, the modern artillery and well-equipped manpower of the fort, but what I mean here is the tide of inevitability, of history. A continental tsunami was on its way, and a few years here or there . . . yeah, neither side could know, least of all imagine. And when I think of which body parts might describe El Paso and the MexAm civilization growing from it, adjectives I'd attach to my more elegant selections would be *potent* and *fertile*.

The next tsunami is a blink away. There is now even more reason to love the West, and intimacy with Mexico will be the plus it should be once we rid ourselves of the ignorant, crude xenophobia of a national Arizona. Time to stare. To be curious. To get smart. At the most western corner of Texas, an old pass tracks the route of our future.

HURRAY FOR LOSERS!

I wrote this in Guatemala, where the very old, the blind or the crippled, still are seen going into the mercado, or selling tortillas near a taxi sitio, or wordlessly begging for quetzales sitting against a wall. Young teenagers often walk with them; all stages of life are visible on ancient streets. I say a writer isn't only the widest reader, smartest, or the best student in a class. Some grow up knowing only the life around them, the jobs available, human struggles and joys. Doesn't mean they don't or can't learn wisdom from stories they've heard or see nor lived in a full life.

AT THE BEGINNING I took auto shop because it didn't make me yawny or sarcastic to be there, and Uncle Willie—what kids called the teacher—might yell now and then, but mostly he left us alone, talking, doing. I liked cars, especially driving them instead of walking or the bus. And better when they were bad-looking. Also for work, yes, but of course there was after work, cruising the starry boulevards, eyeing girls, the summer wind blowing through open windows all year round.

These were the best times, the very best, all the older, mature veterans of life would say. I remember, I listened. None talked college years or the kind of jobs that came after college. All my friends, ones who weren't into glue, or likely headed to county a few times, or fantasizing too much about music careers (because they listened, not out of talent), talked about jobs and income as soon as they got out. Loading docks and trucker training, fireman, bartender, carpenter, plumber, jet mechanic, butcher. I had one high school friend who had come from New Zealand. Poor, his family was set up by the Mormon Church. He planned to go to BYU but, in my mind, that was because it was a Mormon thing, nothing to do with normal world, normal us. Like me. Another friend, a girlfriend, she had a cousin who started college, but when her mom went to Mexico for her sick mother, she had to take care of the family instead. Another friend I made had come from Colorado. The Rocky Mountains. That was impressive to me in itself. He lived with his mom, a secretary at a parts factory. One day his dad came to town. He'd never mentioned him before. His dad, unemployed, was once an engineer. Of course, yes, I thought railroad. I knew older people who worked at the yards. Not that though. And more, he had a master's degree. I didn't know what that was, where it ranked in the educated order. It was out there and up high special, like from another land. One day my new friend got horrible news. His dad had shot himself. I don't think I even asked what kind of weapon, if I only imagined a shotgun. And my friend had to go to his apartment and clean it up. Brains and blood on the wall and floor is all I heard of it that one day he told me, and never again. Educated people were unusual.

Then, tenth grade (though it didn't change in eleventh or twelfth), the only colleges I knew of had headlining football teams. In LA it was USC and UCLA in the sports pages. I didn't know where either of their campuses were, had never seen a campus even, only that they both played at the Coliseum. Nobody I knew of went to a college like that. Actually, any college at all. Excluding the few off-the-books types, people I knew of, older, had jobs in construction, shops, factories, or delivering things in trucks. I had a friend whose mom was an *executive* secretary. A "rich" girl in high school's dad delivered the US Mail. Before she married the one after my dad, my own mom had a job at a dentist's office because she was pretty, not because she knew anything about offices or teeth. She dated lots of culos whose employment I didn't care to learn until she married one that became a temporary stepdad. My dad had worked full-time at an industrial laundry since he was thirteen. I got to start working there the summer I turned fourteen. And during school I worked four hours every day and eight on Saturdays. Most adults I knew and spoke to worked there, all minimum-wage level. About a fourth of them whose origins were the Deep South, who knew about sports in town, the other three-fourths, who didn't follow any college sports local or national, from Mexico and Central America. They of course didn't talk a lot about any high school days, let alone the prep for what came after.

Nobody ever told me to go to college. That I should. Not one adult, in an office or on the street or in my home. Nobody expected me to go to college. Nobody discussed what it took to go to college. I remember—not even sure of the language then—that when asked on a form, like that, I picked college prep as my plan. Maybe it was the other options that were so bad. But the reason, for me, that I picked it was that it was the best choice. The top. Because I was aspiring to be, if not already, an elitist. I wanted more, better, the best possible at whatever it was. I didn't know what that was exactly, or at all, or how you made it happen, but I had confidence in my abilities, whatever they turned out to be once they were in front of me. I liked cars, but no way I wanted to be a mechanic.

I'd say I wasn't as less-than-average as my grades. I got B's in a couple of subjects. Like Spanish. Not an A because a grade wasn't about what you knew only. The teacher wasn't particularly fond of me, and I don't blame him, though he was a bloated fart and deserved me and other pains in the class. I might have gotten A's in PE and auto shop and even math once or twice. Maybe B's. Probably, maybe. Grades weren't about skills. C's in the rest. Except English, where I got at least three or four or even five D's. Not just that I never did homework (I had a job was my excuse)—I never carried a book home, and so I kept having specific trouble with those teachers. The only time I asked for a meeting with a counselor and vice principal (instead of one being called about me) was because I figured out the teacher planned to flunk me. I wanted a transfer to any other class so I wouldn't be held back or have to take it again. She agreed to pass me at the meeting.

My senior year my mom married again and I found a full-time

graveyard shift job as a janitor at McDonnell-Douglas—had to get military-grade government clearance for that, and it came even though I was in high school, had just turned seventeen, and lied. I was allowed to go half-day to a better neighborhood school, because clearly I was so advanced. I wanted the diploma. I always missed my first morning class to have breakfast and slept in the next. The next two classes weren't real classes. They gave a group of the special students like me a special "class" that was like two.

And so I graduated. Like most of my friends did too. I was the only one who pushed on and stuck to it at the community college level. And I was pure lucky. When I first got, for example, an F in a freshman English class (I had no belief that could happen, especially when I was trying—I got D's on papers, and gave up), I soon after received my Please Come to the Induction Center letter in those Vietnam draft days, and I went (not a cheerful place). I visited my draft board office right after and asked if I could have a second chance for a student deferment. And they let me. Working full-time, I took a night class, where I suddenly became smarter, and got a B in that freshman comp course. Well-intentioned, I wasn't close to a high-level student then, but, given information, I was someone who could take what I knew I could do and figure out what came next.

Like me, my friends, all of them, did what they did, what they'd learned, harmlessly almost always. We were the mess-ups. We were the ones who didn't sit in the front of the classroom and join school clubs and organizations and government. Some guys played sports, some girls were on drill team and cheerleaders and a homecoming princess, even a queen, but none of us got the best grades or worried about them, knew one thing about the best schools or even good ones. We were the ones who bought a car that was too expensive and worked to pay it off, to make it cooler, faster, lower, or were losing it to thieves or collection agencies. Ones who took too many drugs, though mostly only *mota*, weed. That got pregnant. That got married too early and had babies too young. That were in love or were trying to do right. Who stayed together or didn't, both full-time occupations. Some jobs were awful, really shitty bosses, or so boring that nobody human, young anyway, could bear it. We tried studying fire science or health care at a junior college and then, oh well. Or business, and no thanks. We worked construction and in department stores or welding and wanted oil pipeline jobs or mining or to go to the wilderness or desert or Mexico and some went kind of hippie or semi-hippie until it was just a job job. Most stayed within a few miles of high school and worked at the familiar here or there, and had rent, lived with someone new and maybe a nice, modest wedding. Or were drafted or joined. Or just had work that came out of the family, lived near all of them. We were they who just did what they'd been doing, what they learned to do.

Little did any of us, they or I, realize that by graduation it was all set. By *all* I mean 99.9 percent. I mean the big shit. The grand, good whole front and backyard, and briefcase dad, and beautifully painted bedrooms like on TV or in movies. I mean, does one exception—which in many ways is me, I'm aware, because, miracle, I became a writer—out of ten thousand (and that's not generous, because isn't it more like a state lottery number?) make a braggable trend? You know, how a certain America rah rah likes to have it. Actually it could have been settled even sooner than that. A bettable wager. Clearly we were traveling on a different American highway than those better behaved than us. And I'm saying there are a lot more of us than those who had a wise father mother grandfather grandmother neighborhood history inheritance and who genetically did everything just right. Better grades, better schools, better family, better manners, better breakfasts, better homework, better birth, better land. Never screwing up. Always hitting it right, with winks and wows coming back at them.

It's not like at first I didn't believe myself that anything was possible. I didn't consider probability, the odds, favorites. I was an elitist to my mind, or at least someone who believed in the better being better, that some can and will do better than others and should. Of course that meant that I could. Maybe I'm too short for an NBA squad, but I could make a major league baseball team! If I'd gone for it. If I'd have thought about it. What I didn't know and couldn't was what I didn't know that I didn't know. In the wide space of anything is possible, I could name like five side-trails and I'd maybe heard of five more. I thought that was a lot—I was doing better than any expectation—and I was off. New York, Paris, Rome, Yale, Harvard? Of course, and sure I heard about all of them! What I knew about was—e.g., South Gate and Watts and Imperial Highway and say the campuses of ELA and Harbor and Compton colleges. Sure I was aware of the biggie deals, of the White House and president and cabinet and their offices, and attorneys and doctors and architects—like I knew of India, the Amazon, like I knew of astronomy, like I knew so many movie stars who lived in LA where I too lived and grew up.

You know these stories well: "At twenty-two he or she accomplished this or that"—and what a job to land on! Admirable greatness, we are left to believe. And we do accept. But . . . by twenty-seven he runs this, controls that, invented, achieved, defended, wrote, and and and. At twenty-two I was still learning to read better, struggling with vocabulary, which is to say my thinking ability, and at twenty-seven I couldn't get a job (by then I had a master's degree in philosophy and religion) but somehow so-and-so didn't have any of that kind of problem ever of any kind. Ever! Not that I don't and didn't believe it, but here's what was really underneath that I was being told to take away from this: They are just smarter. More talented. More ambitious. More skilled. More accomplished and able. Work harder. Super trained. Perfect personality, mesh with the world, with the biz. More fluent, articulate, focused. In sum, the best, they earned it. And I say okay. And I do not believe it isn't true. I am sure it is. Such are the breaks. *Así es.* Life. Whereas. . . .

Here's where the bad kid in me will be sent to the vice principal's office yet again, where my attitude has gotten my butt fired from let's say a number of jobs over the years. Because here comes another list that starts with a *Whereas.* . . .

A step sideways first: I was a construction worker two decades after I received my master's degree. Union high-rises generally. A one-crane job would be like thirty to seventy-five men there, depending on what stage of what. There were always a few Chicano carpenters on downtown jobs, a few mexicanos.* A few more percentage of Black carpenters, especially at the bigger projects, of two or even three cranes. One job I remember, in West LA, they'd had this one apprentice, Black, who didn't work directly with me but was around and who seemed in every way normal and capable from my distance. Who at break would sit with me and another two Chicanos and one drawling tejano and a few laborers—except for the dude from outside Houston, we were all Dodger and Laker fans and the apprentice was too. Then one day he was gone. Let go. The foreman said he was tired of him coming in late and being lazy, that he had too many screw-ups, and that he didn't like his mouth. Like I said, I barely knew the guy, and what the foreman said was all possible, and I didn't give it much more thought. In the trades, jobs came, jobs went. Then there was a layoff. The two mexicano carpenters and the two big, older Black carpenters were given checks. Job slimming down as we got closer to the top seemed like a plausible explanation. Keeping the younger, faster dudes who also could speak English to the boss. Soon enough two new carpenters appeared, both friendly and easy around the foreman. And in a blink a new apprentice too, who seemed connected to the new boys. I had to be around him more, and he wasn't too pleased about that, and I for one didn't enjoy him much either. He was a fucken jerk. If I asked him to do something, he'd frown, like it was beneath him. He was a hothead, got outraged at laborers for not doing what, in fact, should have been his job, wronged if any one of us (not his buddies) suggested that maybe he forgot this, didn't do that well enough—normal

* Two usage comments: (a) throughout this manuscript the word "mexicano" (or "mexicana") will be used to mean a person who in the past was called, in US idiom, a "Mexican national." Back when it was employed to distinguish itself from the word "Mexican," which could also mean a Mexican American. Historically, that word was used with more connotation than denotation. As not so qualified, good enough, and a lot worse. Or, as the character Liz Lemon on an episode of 30 Rock (apocryphally, as in maybe, pretty sure) asked quizzically, "Mexican . . . why does that word sound so racist when I say it?" Here the word will be mexicano, no cap, following Spanish grammatical rules. (b) As to the unending debate about italicizing words from Spanish, when the word is referring to words or phrases being used inside Mexican culture, it will be italicized; if used by Americans inside the US, no italics.

advice for apprentices—and maybe he should buy his own tools so he didn't borrow and lose ours. And he missed days and was late often enough and hungover bad on Mondays. What the boss said? He's young, feeling his oats. His mouth? Fiery, full of spunk. Shitty work? He's learning, how it goes at first.

And so it is for all the special, those treated specially from the special lands. Yet even that can seem sort of like nature's way—power picking what suits it. More money, for instance, goes to those who are living around more money places, and people in the wealthier places have more money to have and choose more. Up to a point anyway, and up to the point when, in a bit of less equanimity, when yet again it's one of them and not one of us, one of me mine, when it's the layoff check here and not there, when it's didn't even get an interview unless it's like Princeton—you know, I could go on and on—and that's when I'm *fuck that! That is what your only 'best' is? Duhhh, gee, every and all the time, huh? You think I don't know better? Do you think I think it's okay? That I'm good with it? Do you really?* And that's when the *Whereas* pops out. Not uttered through the lips, not one word like the following (unless maybe you push, freaking hard, except then you're at a construction site, you're not talking about high, sophisticated power that doesn't have a stupid Trump-like face even thinking it): Whereas you, sir, you are just not our winner kind. Proof? This outburst. We go with winners and winners start as winners. You, sir, are no winner.

Oh god is that true. I grew up in LA and when I got out, I went not to New York or San Francisco, but straight to El Paso, of all places. I didn't even know Princeton was in New Jersey until a few years ago. But you do know I'm not really talking about me, right? I'm not. I'm okay. A lot better than I and anyone who knew me when would have ever imagined. What I am talking about is what I love. America? Sure, lots I am grateful for, my birth here instead of there. And of course what I mean by America includes its history of what is below its southern border, and what I mean is what I have imagined was the best of America, the openness, the range and grandness of space real and dreamed. And the honest prospect of opportunity, not just for the privileged clutter at the top, way over there and all about there.

I'm an elitist. That is, I believe in the best and that it should be admired and learned from and supported. It's just that my own view of best isn't what goes for best in this country of my birth.

A few years ago I was living in Oaxaca, one of the most beautiful cities in México. Every morning I walked down a hill to get a *cafecito*. At a corner, a block up from the café, a lady in a typical Mexican housedress would have set up a table, selling morning chilled *frutas* all cut into cubes and in plastic containers. They were mango, piña, melón, sandía, and sometimes even coconut. My second visit to her I bought two and she suggested that my girlfriend might prefer some limón and chile on the coco. When I told her I was *solito* but especially liked mine that way, she laughed—at sorry me or lucky me, I couldn't tell—and gave me one for free. I went every day and began to sit next to her for an hour to talk and listen and eat a little fruit and hear stories (and learn words and phrases in her native language) and watch people buy her fruit. She always saved me a coco when she brought them. She was Zapoteca, from a village not far, but now lived nearby. Every morning she got up by 4:30 and went to the market and picked out the fruit and hurried back to her home where she cut and boxed them so she could be on the street early.

Almost eighty, she told me this was what she'd learned to do, and she had been doing it for decades, though not always in the same spot. She lived on these pesos from twenty-five to thirty-five fruit boxes. Of course it occurred to me to ask her how it was that she was this. But I couldn't. Couldn't treat her as a subject, a topic. She was more friend, a respected elder, and after a month she treated me, for that hour, as part of her life, sharing. I was already as lucky as I could be, able to be there, the large of it, the small of it. And what else but my luck? My fortune. The big metaphor of that, the small connotation. She was so good, so lively and happy to be living her fate. So quick to talk and to laugh. There could be no better than her, no harder working, ambitious, accomplished. Like pure water. The best. She was just, normally, unseen. A few pesos, a gracias.

In these days, these last decades especially, it's as if privilege is taken for granted by those who live inside it, who don't know a world that is not it—that exotic, other world where there are other, poorer, lesser people who . . . just don't and probably, certainly, didn't have what it takes, weren't born better. Lately, these days, in these years, privilege isn't simply accepted, it's notched more upward and it is assumed it is only true, right. Privilege has made its special more so. It's advancing the special and calling only those therein "the best." And though it could be so, I'm not buying that fruit.

A LITTLE BIT OF FUN
BEFORE HE DIED

Ripley was a pain in everyone's ass. Which, by the way, I often think is a tell in a living being of unique work. He was always hilarious. He was the first writer I ever got to know. Busted for drug dealing (large quantity cocaine, marijuana), his forte, his early release probation was dependent on him being a committed grad student in creative writing at UT El Paso.

ONLY WEEKS BEFORE, I'D been across the street at the University of Texas at El Paso Museum, working a three-story add-on as a carpenter, the second-highest-paid worker on the jobsite at five dollars an hour. It was because I could also tie steel, an ironworker's trade, that I got this big-time wage. No, it was not good money even then, in 1979, except in El Paso. Yes, I was proud of myself to have backdoored my way into an English department teaching job that included a well air-conditioned downstairs office. It really belonged to a full-timer who never used it, and since he liked me, he wanted to help the young writer out. A sweaty carpenter banging nails those weeks ago, now I was banging an electric typewriter, finishing my first novel. I would learn that lots of my new colleagues there didn't really like my having an office. I was only a part-timer—a couple of remedial composition classes I had to learn to teach under the false assumption, theirs, that I had a graduate degree in English. But there I was, a luxurious office completely to myself, with a sweet, picturesque view of the very poorest lean-to shacks of Juárez across the border. Typing. I was not unhappy with the change in my personnel status.

Next door was one of the many and mostly shared offices. I did not socialize much with campus people, so initially I was not very responsive when Bill Ripley, half of my next-door neighbor, interrupted the precious artist-at-work concentration I kept on my first opus. He was a bigger than the numbers six-two. His belly was prominent even then, and that's what I and many called him, too, Belly Ripley. He showed much personal abuse all over his body already, beginning with the acne scars from his youth. I don't remember what his exact first words to me were, how he charmed me, but I am sure it had to do with his country-boy grin, and I'm sure it had something to do with him suggesting how both of us surely needed an afternoon toddy. I had never heard the word "toddy" before, and so I certainly had never had one. So I stepped out with him, persuaded, sold, actually smiling about cutting my afternoon schedule short.

I think the word "toddy" didn't only make me want to laugh in itself. It was the way Ripley made the word's fussiness sound even funnier, especially as it echoed in an air-conditioned hall at the Texas Mexican border. It was so, like, Eastern—at once both sophisticated and classy, yet mocking that pretension. Like drinking hot tea in tea cups and saucers with those rings in the middle to secure the cup there and teaspoons (as in, spoons for tea) for, I guess, a lump of sugar. Or honey. Or maybe to stir milk? I hadn't been taught any of this in my youth. El Paso was the most east I'd ever lived.

Whereas Ripley, with his Texas drawl, he'd gone to Harvard. I knew what Harvard was like I knew what the White House was. President Kennedy went to Harvard. Ripley was the first person I ever met and talked to—had a toddy with, which he taught me was just a shot of whiskey at a bar—who'd gone to Harvard.

Not only that, Ripley'd published his first short story in the *Harvard Crimson*, the campus paper. Which was all the more impressive to me, since he thereby became the first person I hung out with who'd ever published anything. He'd turned down a scholarship offer, he told me, to play football at Texas. After Harvard, he got into a law school—I think in Colorado—but he hated law school and loved drugs and therefore lasted only a week, give or take. He moved to Austin. He had title, he would say, to some iddy-biddy acres there in central Texas, which, like anyone else who'd never been east of El Paso, I assumed was lots of dirt, not what I know now to be Dripping Springs, which is twenty miles west of Austin, in the idyllic Texas Hill Country. He began to sell marijuana on a larger scale than many, moving it out of West Texas to the north and east. He had three women drivers who, he claimed, listened to him attentively and loved his cocaine. Women, he explained, were the best drivers because the cops never suspected them. When one of them got pulled over with a few hundred pounds of weed, his theory was proven to be mistaken. Except his stepdaddy was a congressman in Colorado, and he knew a lawmaker in El Paso. His conviction was adjudicated unto a sentence of him never leaving the city limits of El Paso without permission while enrolling himself in a master's degree program in creative writing at UTEP.

I knew nothing about creative writing. Until that point, despite evidence everywhere which apparently didn't register in my brain, I thought all writers were dead—not their literature, only them—and therefore I had a good shot at some openings. For years, I was the only living person I was conscious of who wrote. What I knew of the contemporary writing business came out of a used copy of *Writer's Market*. In El Paso, with my new job, my outlook was transmogrifying. I had even befriended a much-praised, published poet and teacher who introduced me to Gary Snyder when he visited. We had dinner together at a small table! I watched and heard a spectacular Robert Bly reading—way before his men's movement fetish and probably before that drum-beating-in-a-circle thing. And the faculty at UTEP, my "colleagues," included Raymond Carver. Now there was Ripley: my first fiction-writer role model.

I liked knowing men who were older than me, because I liked learning from them, and so I liked Ripley, even when I wasn't always comfortable with him. First of all, despite being a large landowner in central Texas (he'd sell an acre now and then when he needed cash), he was always broke and mooching. He would often slump his big shoulders and virtually pull out the pockets of his pants right when he got to the cash register with a bottle of whiskey, looking at me like a puppy dog. I didn't really like whiskey, and though I plead guilty to drinking more of it than I ever had in my life, he drank three to my one. I lived in an apartment with only a wife, a double mattress on the floor we shared, a rocking chair, a TV (black and white), and a newborn baby who shared the rocking chair with her and the mattress with both of us. This was the entire expanse of our belongings besides here and there clothes and books. I barely made the monthly rent, and that was with construction side jobs I did.

Along with Ripley's busty girlfriend, who he called Peaches or Cookies or Creamy—I can't remember—we were once asked to leave a late-night Denny's. They'd been eating their food with too much wet, licking spoons and chewing on forks, too drunk and high, and I did laugh too loud myself too. Though I'd concede that the noise at our table didn't help, in my opinion the heap of staring was out of a visual taboo—his petite girlfriend, who was in her early twenties, looked fifteen and would often be taken for his daughter if left without an introduction, while he, being overindulgent in every category of intake, had more middle-aged bulk, and his other excesses prematurely lined his face into that of a man in his midforties. Not that the two of them couldn't in fact offend. Back in his apartment, little Peachie might jump on his stuffed chair, straddle his lap, and pull up her top so that he could nibble and suckle. I had to tell Ripley that, nice as that seemed even from my distance, could he please take me home?

Numbers of events in his El Camino. I had to tell him often to be careful when he spoke about Mexicans. Always uncomfortable with his cracker side, I would steam about his favorite racial descriptives. When I'd blow, he'd say I was crazy and exaggerating and being overly sensitive. Once he was driving and another car did something he didn't appreciate. Niggers, he yelled, though none were Black. I had to tell him: Let's be clear, Ripley. You ever have a problem with any Black dudes because you just said that, I'm telling you now I do not and will not back you up. You are on your own, and I will make it very well-known whose side I'm on.

He could only shake his big head and go like it was me making something of nothing, not getting his humor, while I would wonder what I was doing riding with him. I didn't drink whiskey and I didn't like shitkickers. Maybe it'd be considered exciting to be moving at a hundred mph, bouncing high off the small rises on Mesa, that big westside El Paso street, but I was never drunk enough to not think it was way stupid and beg him to stop. Like slowing through red lights and stop signs, driving too fast was his deal. Maybe the draw for me was that Harvard mix in it: He was going maybe forty-five through Kern Place—a desirable, rich, attractive Anglo neighborhood—and ahead not fifty yards, on the left side of the street, a yardman in a straw hat was raking leaves. Without losing any speed, Ripley steered that El Camino and ran it over the curb and onto the middle of the lawn and into a stop exactly beside the man who could not have moved fast enough. He rolled down his window. As stunned as I was as a passenger, the mexicano clutched the rake. His mouth might not have been open even if it seems like it was to my memory. I swear he didn't blink. I, too, would have thought I had just survived death were I him. And then, as he did, I started listening to Ripley lecturing on the topic of life's sorrows and expectations after retirement from sports. The yardman, who I don't think was following a word of it even if he knew enough English, didn't move, didn't flinch, made no sound whatsoever. It certainly was not as hilarious as it hit me, drunk enough, but I was crying with shameless and shameful laughter.

Laughter. Laughing was how we wrote a poem one afternoon at a relatively new gourmet-style coffee shop on Mesa Street. Ripley was in a graduate class in poetry and had to write a poem. He didn't write poetry and, no, I certainly could not help him—never an attempt at verse ever. "Come on, Dagoberto." There was always something funny, humor-inducing, about Ripley even saying my name. It alone caused me to grin. Maybe how he made each syllable a drawled word of badly accented Spanish. He wrote a line. I shook my head. Then we had to talk and figure until we started laughing about what we were trying to do—you know, scamming out a poem for a class to keep his parole grades up—and it got so that what the poem should be about was us doing this. That is, not working, drinking, high, creating poetry, more cheating on "homework" than making art.

Which was the art of it! As true poets, he'd pronounced us, we were so often so very busy "researching" for serious art that it was demeaning to have to write obligatory poetry for a class.

Therefore, it wasn't fair. He'd write a line about life not being fair. Once a line made us both laugh, it became a keeper, and more lines piled up. It got so that, toward the end, we were laughing way out of control. A funny poem, the fun, much of it off the page, was that we were writing this at all, and editing it through laughing. We were just messed up, until finally he was downing coffee to get sober enough to type it up and submit it to his early-evening seminar.

The poem was about us sitting there in an air-conditioned coffee shop, in the middle of a scorching desert afternoon in El Paso, having nothing but poetry to do, while everybody else out there in the world was responsibly employed. All we wanted to do—all we had to do—was to have a little bit of fun. That was what Ripley always said, like it was his motto or creed. Especially when he was Rippedly, wasted on drugs or liquor, usually both, which was a lot. Funny, Ripley was a sad, self-destructive, self-abusing man. And when he was really too fucked up, so gone his mass became a limp blob of can-barely-move, he might get his breath too close to my face, and in his most insincere voice, say, "Dagoberto, all I want to do is have a little bit of fun before I die. Now is that too much to ask for? Is it?"

• • •

By the mid-80s, I was the father of a second son and I'd joined the union in Los Angeles as a Class A high-rise journeyman carpenter. Now I wrote short stories. I thought once I'd published a few, agents or publishers would believe in me as a writer and want that novel I'd finished in El Paso, which I didn't realize yet was simply lousy. I mean, they were in love with Raymond Carver, and if they wanted working class, well, I actually was still working in that working class more years than I wished I had to.

We lived in a duplex near Micheltorena that overlooked Sunset Boulevard. Next to the building was an empty lot that descended from our street curb down to the sidewalk along Sunset. It was ground-covered in ivy. Which is a jungle paradise for rats. During the fall, it rained so much that the rats were running openly all around in front of our narrow street to get out of their flooded nests. It was sick. I went after disgusting rats like a serial killer. I wrote a story called "The Rat" and I sent it to the literary magazine *Quarterly West*. It was Ripley who turned down the story, saying something like it wasn't him but the rest of them who didn't like Mexicans or literary fiction about them. He'd moved on too. After he'd finished a master's degree in creative writing at UTEP, he went for a PhD in creative writing at the University of Utah.

It wasn't too long after that he was in LA doing a tiny drug transaction, which also coincided with him getting an opportunity to visit his buddy James Crumley, who was in Hollywood to write a screenplay of his novel *The Last Good Kiss* for the director Robert Towne. Crumley had briefly become a creative writing teacher at UTEP right after I left, and as part of their bonding and mentoring, he and Ripley drank, and so on, a lot. No, not only did I not mind him so wasted when I agreed to drive him to visit Crumley that Saturday afternoon, I was outright excited. At its most lucrative, my life consisted mostly of getting to construction sites by six in the morning and putting in ten or more. When would I ever get to see what it looked like to be put up free in a posh hotel as a writer? But try as I might to finally leave once we'd been there long enough, Ripley sipping more and more, Crumley insisted that Ripley could not be left there. I didn't blame Crumley, but I wasn't expecting to have to care for Ripley the rest of the day either. What else could I do but drive him to the last place he'd been?

Sometime before, my wife had been telling me that she thought there'd been a rat in her car, which was a fifteen-year-old Chevy Nova. She showed me our baby's car seat as evidence. I saw how some of its upholstery was shredding at a seam, but I thought there was some other explanation and didn't take it seriously. I was driving Ripley in the Chevy because it was the more luxurious of our poor cars. Ripley was aiming for stupor by the time we left Crumley, and I wasn't especially thrilled. I was afraid he'd gotten the address of the next place we were going wrong, and I would be stuck with his bloat for many more hours. I remember making turns assertively, just, you know, because. If I turned left, the Rippedly would bounce against the passenger door. If I went right, he tipped over to hit my shoulder. I was on the Hollywood Freeway, probably sighing because now I didn't even have anyone to talk to—though I was always tired because of construction work—when I felt his fingers scratching my left shoulder. When I turned my head to him to ask what the fuck, he was drooling with his eyes closed, slumped against the passenger door. I turned my head toward the windshield and felt, then saw, the rat quickly clawing down my left arm, which was attached to the steering wheel. My window was up, but the wind wing was open, turned to allow wind in always because a thief had broken it off its upper hinge and it dangled from the bottom. Ripley! I yelled.

The rat jumped from my wrist to the top of the driver's side windowsill. Ripley! I yelled. He moaned. The rat scooted to the wind-wing opening. Ripley, look! He moaned. The rat held itself there for between one and two seconds, pondering, looking left and right, down at the strobe of the white lane stripes, who knew? And it dove onto the Hollywood Freeway. Ripley, did you see that?! "What, Dagoberto?" That rat, the rat that just jumped out! "Come on, Dagoberto." I'm telling you! I yelled. "Dagoberto, you have rat on your brain." Drunk, he did not believe me. Sober, he never did either, as many times as I recounted that amazing, disgusting rat suicide.

* * *

Tales of Ripley accumulated. One had him in central Texas driving wild in the country, with open beers and empty cans in his vehicle, and when he pulled over to pee, he was swarmed and arrested by the Secret Service. President George Herbert Walker Bush was quail hunting nearby. Another had him in Utah at a party where it was either Rust Hills, fiction editor of *Esquire*, or Gary Fisketjon, editor of the new Atlantic Monthly Press, drunk and cocained, who battled him in a groveling contest. As Ripley explained, it involved the two crawling across the room to see who was more wasted. When he didn't make it there first, Ripley told Fisketjon that the winner of a groveling contest was he who couldn't get there. The biggest news: He exclaimed that he had been given a book contract by Atlantic Monthly Press. To me, it was his funniest creative writing achievement ever.

Ripley had taken the stories he had written for a master's degree and linked those into a novel, a creative "dissertation," to earn a PhD and what became *Prisoners*, his only book. Yet as the sales of the publication faded quickly, so did Ripley. No more fellatio-obsessed fictions by him, only more sorry tales of him multiplied, and then he was busted traveling from Texas on his way to Colorado, holding, a large quantity, sales, along those lines. He was weeks in a local jail before his family bailed him out.

But what became the oddest Ripley event ever began back while he was in Utah. I don't know if he had published any previous short stories, but one did appear in the first volume of a series titled *The Best of the West*. In the story, some of the poem that Ripley and I laughed into existence became the opening of this mediocre short story (a Dagoberto character became a snake handler, something like that). What I heard was that it was published because his reputation was consuming Utah. Since I was a figure in his lore, therefore I, too, seemed to have earned some strange cachet. Which was the only explanation I could come up with for why, one day back in El Paso—where I, my sons, and wife had returned after Los Angeles—I received a poetry manuscript for a blurb. By that date, the later 1980s, I had published lots of short fiction but only a chapbook-size collection of stories, the first book from a new small press in El Paso. I'd never been asked to blurb anything, and anyone asking had to be suspicious. And this was the galleys of a poetry collection due out soon from a well-known press. The author, Wyn Cooper, someone I'd never met or even heard mention of, was a young poet, a grad of the Utah program, a protégé I assumed, smitten by the romance of Ripley's debauchery.

The only poem that stood out to me, "Fun," I remember well, a liveliness and color and style not in the others, was about Ripley. I left the volume near my bookcase.

Years passed. I'd estimate it was near a decade that I didn't have the slightest inclination to speak to or contact Ripley because I was so pissed off at some business we'd done. I'd hear of him once in a while, sightings and tales, but it was thanks to my friend, the author of *Afoot in a Field of Men*, Pat Ellis Taylor (who changed her name to Pat Little Dog), a woman's Kerouac, famous all over Austin, whose book was published and promoted alongside Ripley's by the same publisher, that I found forgiveness. Pat did many kinds of the lowest-paying jobs to earn a living and write poetry and live in humid apartments. During the Fourth of July period, she'd open up a fireworks stand. She and her partner would clean out abandoned buildings and suites from failed businesses, and they'd sell the used wares along the side of the highway. One of her more steady gigs was the annual gathering of TAAS test readers and graders. The TAAS test system (Texas Assessment of Academic Skills) was Texas Governor George Bush's way to test public-school students, and it panicked almost everyone whose job it was to teach the young. The Republicans, in particular, believed these tests would make the schools, rich or poor, accountable, and they were particularly proud. What no one talked about were the test graders, an overeducated social caste, most of them habitually underemployed or unemployable, who saw TAAS as major seasonal income, after which they could return to their various drug addictions, alcoholisms, manias, phobias, severe depressions, marijuanismos, general unsuitablenesses, and plain weirdnesses. And so it was that Pat Little Dog, regular TAAS grader and reader, told me she had actually sat next to and lunched with Bill Ripley during TAAS grading, where they laughed about their literary success. She told me Ripley said to say hi to me. I once again smiled about Rippedly. I was over it. I told her to say I said hello back. I told her to give him my phone number.

Not too much later, I found Ripley living in a moldy dump in a complex in South Austin. His roommate had been recently released from a penal facility. Ripley had become Dr. Ripley, "The Dark Professor," he called himself. He wrote school papers for a business that catered to loser students who would pay well for them. He liked literary topics the best. His specialty was to offer original compositions that could never be resold. He could also write a B-range paper upon request—sometimes, he explained, suspicions could arise if, suddenly, a student got too smart. But, he said, he was a doctor of creative writing, and he could write in any voice, any style that was desired. Lately, he'd gotten to sounding a little paranoid. Working for one of the athletic programs at UT Austin, he heard that somebody thought he saw Ripley geezing outside, or in the bathroom, something like that. Ripley was worried because, maybe, they were a little concerned about what he knew and what he did and what he might say if they let him go, but how much worse if they didn't. And so on.

I hadn't visited him in a long time, but I was making a better-than-average-wreck of my own life, an okay time for me to share in his latest troubles. It seemed that the singer Sheryl Crow, living in Los Angeles, was having writer's block, so to help her out, her producer visited a few used bookstores and bought some poetry books. The producer picked out the one I hadn't blurbed, the one that had the poem "Fun" in it. It was that poem that cured her. She wrote "All I Wanna Do." Though she placed the setting off Santa Monica Boulevard, and Ripley's name itself gets inside her lyrics with an evaluation of him, you can still see the "verses," or the ideas in them, he and I laughed at off Mesa Street even layered through Cooper's poem.

"All I want is to have a little fun
Before I die," says the man next to me
Out of nowhere, apropos of nothing. He says
His name's William, but I'm sure he's Bill
Or Billy or Mac or Buddy; he's plain ugly to me,
And I wonder if he's ever had fun in his life.

We are drinking beer at noon on Tuesday,
In a bar that faces a giant car wash.
The good people of the world are washing their cars
On their lunch hours, hosing and scrubbing
As best they can in skirts and suits.

Ripley was sunk deep into a stuffed couch, books and papers puddled all around, and it was almost like there was a film noir detective lamp on him. His face was liquid and sticky-looking, the Texas sweat had caked but was still moist, his graying hair more afraid to relax than simply uncombed and messy, the REM-like flutter of his eyes so quick that human ones like mine took their movement as too slow. His voice was calm, each syllable as distinguishable as the one that preceded and the one which would follow. He'd reached a new dimension of wasted.

"All I Wanna Do" was a hit everywhere, even number one in Germany, as Ripley kept pointing out as dramatic proof of something more. When the rights for the poem were first bought, his excited friend Cooper, Ripley wanted me to believe, offered to pay him half. He wanted to, Ripley claimed, because Cooper always said the poem was Ripley's, too. And Ripley agreed, but since it was only a couple thousand dollars, he wouldn't take half that. "He was a friend, Dagoberto, and Cooper wouldn't take that little bit from a friend." He was happy for him then. But now? Why wouldn't he give him some now? He didn't even want half anymore. Just a cut. Fifteen percent was a fair amount, he thought. Cooper refused. He would give nothing. Ripley began to read aloud a too-long and boring letter he had written Cooper, explaining friendship, their friendship, their poem, their agreement according to him. It was a painfully bad letter, the worst Ripley creative writing I'd ever heard.

There was a pounding on the door. Bang, bang, bang. A fist mocking Ripley's speech pattern. He got up like a weightlifter straining for the record. The visitor was a shady dude whose eyes darted. Ripley went through another door and came back. He had the prettiest colita of marijuana you'd ever seen, all curled cute inside a clear freezer bag. The dude, who did not seem like someone into weed, smelled it and rubbed it between his fingers, bought it. When he left, Ripley plopped back into the stuffed couch. He asked if I wanted or knew anyone who wanted an ounce or two of crystal meth. He didn't think so, he said, but he had to ask.

We actually heard the song playing on a radio outside an open window. It was impossible to not laugh. He didn't know what he should do. Ripley said he'd gotten his uncle in Corpus Christi to pursue Cooper. Ripley's uncle was an intellectual property lawyer. At that time, I didn't even know there was such an item, let alone an attorney for it. Then Ripley clutched what I remember—surely wrong—looked to me like a telegram. It was, Ripley told me, from Cooper or his representative, or his uncle, like that, and said that unless he ceased and desisted in his demands, like that, he would be exposed as a drug dealer and heroin addict. Ripley looked at me like I should be as astounded as he was by the charge. "Why would he be this way, Dagoberto? Why would he want to say these things about me?" I shook my head. What could I add but my laughter?

I didn't keep in touch with Ripley. I have no clue how much fun he had left in him before he died, seven years ago, though he did find a woman and they moved to California. Years passed. Ten more? I got one email from him from there and it was all in caps. It wasn't really screaming at me, being loud, but the opposite. He said he was happy.

THOU SHALT NOT STEAL
BOOKS

I was asked to write this to support the Santa Barbara Public Library. I wanted it to be my apology for having such bad habits learned in my youth.

I WASN'T A BOOK boy. I did have a child's picture book of *Moby Dick*. Probably twenty-five words a page, very colorful drawings, thirty big pages total? My favorite, and only. I loved it. I have no idea how it got in my possession. I didn't steal it, I say to assure you. Books weren't an item in my home. I remember I did like the glossy-cover encyclopedias they sold, I think it was weekly (could have been monthly), in the supermarkets way back then. I'd persuaded my mom to buy one or two or even three. I never really read them, just liked the idea of them and getting smart if you had them around. I might read a sports page. Mostly scores and stats of especially baseball. I played sports. Whatever was around, whatever anybody wanted to play. I was good at that.

Things changed right after high school. By that I mean for and in me. These were the Vietnam years. Hippies, weed, mushrooms, all as common as long hair (acid seemed to be for nerdy or loony whiteboys who didn't need jobs or come from where they mattered) and those drafted and going, or finally back but a touch wacko and scary. I'd read a book my senior year— by that I mean I tried to—because I was in this special two-hour flunky

English class for those of us they had to do something with. I thought the teacher was a drunk. Nobody and not me either in this class cared and that's why we were in it. One day this man told those who were listening (or overhearing? I can't remember him talking like a teacher) that hippies read a book called *Stranger in a Strange Land*, that it was like the hippie bible. I don't know where I got it (the teacher maybe?) but I don't believe I stole it. I wanted to learn about hippies because I liked marijuana and music and . . . all that seemed pretty nice about their cute girls and easy life. I didn't get the book at all, what it was about, and I never heard the word "grok" with any of the people I encountered then or ever. But I did like that I'd read a book (even if I don't think I did, really, at least most of it). It made me feel smarter and that seemed . . . well, good. In the land I'd come up in, it was stupid sucks (the worst of them big and pissed off for being ugly), into scamming or gaming something, and mostly drunk or getting there. I wanted smart.

And so it was either Vietnam or, to stall, junior college. I didn't grow up with my father, a WWII Marine sergeant, but even he, I learned, like many, wasn't sure it was a wise move to be a draftee and go there. I kept my full-time employment and went to community college. It was like discovering girls for me. And my world flipped. There wasn't a class I came into knowing anything. I was starving for it all. And I wanted to read the books for class cover to cover. Slow at first, word after word looked up, graph to page to chapter to one after another. There followed books that weren't assigned. Then books others told me about. Then ones I found out about. Books that led to more books.

By the time I transferred to UC Santa Barbara, I thought I was a full-fledged intellectual. I wanted a revolution. I wanted a few. And I stole books. That had nothing to do with a revolution, since I used to steal shit when I didn't know that word and it was candy or beer or gin or albums—those were the gentle things. But it did help to justify it that I was, uh, stealing for the revolution and not me me me. They weren't often even anything to do with revolution. Of course I read Marx, Hegel, Marcuse and Fanon, the Soledad Brothers, Wright, Cleaver. I would steal Camus, Rulfo, Hesse, Paz, Beckett, and Dostoyevsky. Once even Porter (I saw all the pretty English majors carrying around her bestselling collection). Mostly it became stranger books. Because real fast I started changing too. I found I liked all kinds of subjects and titles. Plato to Chuang-tzu to García Márquez and so on. And I wanted everything I read. What is that? That want to own *that* book you read, like it's *yours*?

I went to UC Santa Barbara my junior year. My favorite bookstore was the Isla Vista Bookstore. I preferred used books, and it had the best-quality ones. I spent hours there learning its sections, trying ones in Spanish, trying ones in French. I got into mass-market westerns, my keeper favorites those where the lead character was an Indian and particularly a half-breed, my specialty. I was such a regular I'd often go there and find a new subject or book and read right there. Sometimes I didn't steal, though mostly that could be seen as strategy—buy one or two real cheap, pants an expensive one or two. And so it was that there was this one pleasant day I'd come in and was wandering around, checking spines and then back covers and a few interior pages. I don't remember where I was, what section, which books. It must have been in a more open area than I usually was. The bookstore had an upper floor that surrounded the main floor, like a gigantic, railed, overhead shelf, where we patrons never went. And maybe I'd been getting so comfortable in there, so used to doing what I did, that I forgot where I was and what I was doing wasn't good: Two books down my pants and I looked up (was something said, or all nonverbal alarms?) and the owner was glaring at me. I felt like we knew each other, we approved of each other. I loved his bookstore. So much of my intimate time there. He couldn't help liking me too—he was a bookstore owner; I was the epitome of who and what they were for. Except the stealing part.

I always thought he was Japanese. I don't mean that to imply he was Zen, something as silly as that. Only a California type that did things well and thoughtfully and wasn't messed up as . . . people like me. He didn't start screaming or calling me names or yelling about police or arrest, didn't rush down to shake or lecture me and cause me to run like a fool. He just stared at me calmly and spoke in a normal voice. "Never come back here again," he said sternly.

I put the stolen books back on their shelf. I creeped off, eyes down, a sicko. I was truly ashamed. And devastated by the loss. I wasn't sure what to do next, where to hide (I couldn't even walk that block for years, pass by), where to be me. I was 50 percent books, both mind and body.

How many hours or days later I don't remember, but I was in downtown Santa Barbara. I didn't go there so often, just easy to drive to the "city" (I came up in the city of LA) and there was a Mexican restaurant with chilaquiles which always cheered me up. After, I was walking. Not a big town, Santa Barbara was a romantically beautiful one. And I got to what is probably its prettiest public space (as in a-thousand-years-later antiquity, its monumental center), the courthouse, museum, library. You know how it is when you're walking in the remnants of ancient cities. You sense time and history, your own life in a larger perspective.

I'd never been a book boy young. Back then libraries to me were field trips, where teachers took you every so often and I had to go and, there, be told to shut up. I walked into Santa Barbara's library. There were kind people at desks offering to help me out. Like nurses, or Franciscans blessing this animal, who was me. These library places were still and calm because there was reading going on. People reading, learning, from books. Obvious, right? I know, that simple unless you'd never paid close attention with your brain. For me it was as if I walked into a cathedral, and a sweet hum of wind light was in my ears and turned my eyes both upward and inward.

Okay, that last part didn't happen thus or at all or with sound effects or a light show. Nothing mystical. But I was cured. I mean, I didn't like that I stole books. I stopped. Never again. Like that part of my stupid life was done. Coincided, a little, with me needing to use libraries with stranger books than any bookstore would or could have. My love of books and bookstores and especially IV Bookstore (I'm still ashamed, my penance this) blew up—expanded—to libraries great and small. I've read in a lot of them now, too. Not just UCSB's or UCLA's, not just Santa Barbara's, but ones in El Paso, Austin, Albuquerque, New York, Stanford, the Library of Congress, all these hexagons (what Borges called them) an entrance to an embracing homeland, where I am both innocent and mature over and over, where, good day or bad, sure or confused, I can always imagine I am going to heaven.

FATHER CLOSE, FATHER FAR

For years after my book The Magic of Blood and an essay in The New Yorker were published, I'd get negative remarks from, you know, certain kinds, about why I didn't talk about the other half of my mestizaje breeding as I do as my mami side. It didn't seem to matter to them that I didn't know much about my dad other than he was a Marine in the war and he met my mom where he worked for what turned out to be forty-nine years, and she lived in the casita next to that job, her mom, my grandmother, being the boss's side mistress.

THE ONLY MEMORY OF my father in what was my home was him leaving it. I remember the event not by its amount of time, whether it took five minutes or some hours, and not for some emotional, psychological cliché. It imprinted because I knew I was supposed to care, and I didn't. It was that he was saying goodbye, that he was leaving the house. What was strange for me was that he was there at all. His presence in the house was where my attention focused, because up to that moment, I wasn't even aware of his existence. I can say, chemically testing the memory now, that I even grasped then the sentimental importance of it. That might only be because my mother was hovering anxiously and I picked up on it. He said something. I doubt it was much. I'm sure it was something reassuring in some gruff sort of way. "Gruff" might be superimposing now, and, even if, how slick could anyone, man or woman, expect to be under the circumstance? I do remember it was supposed to mean something, I could tell. It just didn't to me. I don't know if that says he hadn't yet lodged himself in some deep psychic part of my life, or ever would, whether he should have, or could have, whether anyone my age then would have acted better or worse or the same, whether it reflects more what is my own nature. But there it is, primally established. I couldn't have been much past three years old, tops.

My father became a distant mythical figure, more force than man. Though nothing Old Testament, he was what my mother would use as a threat of wrath and punishment. Not that it had altered any wildness I was being criticized for, and in a short time I would learn this was only a feint, easily dismissed. He was a little Old Country to me—I would make visits like on three days a year, which were really just a few hours to have to tolerate—but that could easily have been only in contrast to my mother, who was congenitally young in style and behavior. I did know a couple of things about him that made him uniquely strong and tough to me: One, that he'd been a Marine sergeant in World War II, a scout in the Pacific islands advanced out to locate Japanese camps, and two, that he'd quit going to school at thirteen to work and, except for the time in the military, he'd never stopped. That became forty-nine years of employment, from 5:30 a.m. to 5:30 p.m. six days a week, until he was laid off.

Where he worked was an industrial laundry—what he called "the plant"—in downtown Los Angeles, near the corner of Washington and Vermont. My mother had grown up next door to it with her mother, my grandmother who died when my mom was a teenager, in what in Spanish would be considered *la casa chica* of one of the two owners of the laundry who my father worked for. That is to say, my grandmother was his mistress and not his wife. I was still thirteen the summer I started working there too. I was excited about it because I wanted to have money, even if I was scared and intimidated the first days I was there. I had to be moving fast by six in the morning, and I had to work beside full-grown men. I was also getting paid the same as them, and though my father didn't say much to me, he told me to never tell them what I made, never show anyone my paycheck. There were basically five large areas to work: sorting, washing, folding, sewing, and loading. I was put in the sorting room in the beginning, where cloth sacks of soiled laundry would be dumped on the cement floor, gathered around, and sorted out into wooden bins with wheels. If it was from a hotel, it was sheets and pillowcases. Restaurants had napkins and tablecloths and grease rags and aprons. The big jobs were hospitals, with sheets, pillow cases, and surgical greens of all kinds, often caked or gelatined with blood. My first days I learned where maggots grew and how to get used to the hot stink of all class of rot. Most of the sorting room men—there were no women on this floor, and no White people whatsoever—were from Mexico but also a few from Central American countries and a third were Black dudes, a couple of whom at first scared the shit out of me—one by his massive size, the other his conked, do-ragged hair—but who I came to like too much, just as I grew to not be the least uncomfortable around the most flamboyant gay Mexican I've never seen the likes of since. When he walked from one end of the room to, say, the toilet, the whole crew, plus or minus thirty men, whistled and hooted as he swished with such fun, calypso exaggeration, grinning like he was on his own runway, modeling the tightest pedal pushers.

There were eight hours a day, six days a week, for loud talk and loud laughter, crazy stories of petty and felony crime, jail and prison, scams and deals, virility and fertility, stupors and raging highs, gossip and slanders, and sometimes there'd even be singing, solos and group harmonies. And so the day would pass, not much like how people talk the bad of having to have a fucking job, once you overlook the part that it was minimum wage, until a guy near one of the garage-size doorways would make those Mexican chirps to warn us he was nearby or coming through: *He* being the boss, the floor super, that is, my dad. Then it would get quiet and go all business. He would enter, a fast and muscular walk, through one doorway and follow a looping path to the other doorway, eyes like a reptile, and be gone. Maybe a couple of times he stopped and talked to a foreman. You didn't even hear his voice, and you knew it was nothing but business. And so, at the job, what I knew of him was still as a mythical creature, more force than human being, the one who brought the checks on Thursday, who once in a while would bring a second, last check on Friday if he wasn't happy about some employee whose time had come. Though I was sure the men thought otherwise, I knew as little about him, personally or otherwise, as they did. Without impunity, before the morning whistle and after the end of the day, I did, if I wanted to, get to go behind the metal countertop that divided the path to the plant's interior, the time-clock path that all workers took to punch in and out, the card slipped into a slotted rack on one side of it or the other. I could even sit in the wooden swivel chairs by the rolltop desk. I had seen things he did that the others couldn't—watching the unemployed—all from México or Central America—coming in asking for work, him telling most of them *no hay nada hoy* except the rare time when, for reasons mysterious and random to me, he'd have a job not moments after he'd said no to someone else, telling this man or that woman to be there in the morning. He was the boss.

I loved that I had my own money, and I worked my two summers of junior high until in high school, after I quit football and track (could not bear the coaches yelling), I also started working four hours after school and all day on Saturday, taking a bus until I could drive myself. I lived with my mom and all her melodramas, while my father I only knew bossing at the plant. I'd been moved from the sorting room to the even bigger floor, where all the mangles steamed, dried, and pressed the sheets and tablecloths and napkins, where mostly women, around seventy-five of them, worked. Hot as it was all the time, I liked it there. One other person, Felipa, had been at the plant a few years longer than my dad, and her partner, María, only a few years less, and they, like many, even knew my mom. People always saved me the best tacos ever made that, rolled up and wrapped in foil, they'd heat up near the gas flames at the back of the giant industrial dryers. I was almost seventeen when, one day, my father came up to me and pulled me aside and suggested my hair was too long. I felt like I was against a wall. Up to that point, we'd never had one intimate conversation, disagreeable or pleasant, not even when I had to visit him at his home one of those nights a year I was expected to. Nothing much more than please pass the mustard, and I like the Dodgers. All else, if anything, was listening, tolerating, waiting to go home. I did not think my hair was too long, and really it wasn't, and what did it have to do with him anyways? But I didn't say so. I nodded my head, and we went back to our work. A day or two later I called in, lied and told him I found a new job, closer to home, and said thanks.

I really didn't see my father much from then, even began disregarding the assumed obligatories (Christmas Eve, his birthday), until many years later. I'd moved north of LA for college and moved to El Paso and then back again, and eventually had my own family. I thought it would be good for my sons to meet their other grandparents—I myself hadn't known any. In my non-adult years, I believed I had descended from a rich man. That was only because when I visited him those days, I surmised that, not just for occasions but every single day, his wife and their daughter and he ate at a dinner table, and there might even be bowls with vegetables, like peas and green beans and carrots, even if they did come out of a can—I considered this the praxis of the rich. Also, he always drove a Cadillac, which maybe he got new, I didn't know. I bought into that image like all dumb peoples who don't know better. It was his front, what he wanted projected. Rich people did drive Cadillacs, in fact, and from the streets, nobody really could know otherwise, especially workers at the laundry, who, like me, saw him with wheels like the owners. They drove Cadillacs too, though maybe they were Lincolns, until finally they rolled in a Mercedes.

• • •

When he died, I didn't expect anything. Aside from the fact that he didn't really know me or, as far as I knew, particularly like me or how I lived or turned out, or that we weren't close whatsoever, even if there was something of his I should have had, a memento, say, I didn't think of that, and even now wouldn't think it was necessary. I mean that in the kindest way, too. I understood the relationship. Besides, he had a wife. When he married her, she was around twenty-three, he was almost fifty. She'd come to LA from Memphis, was even a second cousin to Elvis Presley (her mom a Presley).

Twenty-five years later she was much the same as she was then, with ridiculously long red polished fingernails, which paralleled the thin, fragile tall she was. She was always drinking a Coke with a bendable straw, smoking Virginia Slims, digesting prescription pain pills—while at the wheel she tore it up, every ride a race she won. What she drove just before his death was an older Datsun sedan. After he'd been laid off, my father earned a commercial real estate agent's license. But over the next ten years he only sold one significant piece of property, and with his cut, probably expecting more to come, he went in all cash for a new Eldorado, banking maybe $2,000 that remained. Nothing more came.

Now his wife had the very low-mileage Cadillac, and she was selling the Datsun. Our best car was a Chevy Nova that had seen its best days. As unimpressive as her Datsun was, it was much better than the Nova. I have to admit that the word *family* occurred to me then, though more like a card played in a board game. Like an earnest word they used on TV shows. It was a word that I only applied to my own wife and children, nothing beyond. If I had family like others talked about it, this was maybe my mom, and she was married to someone, and even that was, to me, about her life. I'd never asked for anything from him ever. Not a loan, nothing. I wouldn't have considered him if I'd ever thought I needed one—not to mention that the answer would've been no. Besides, I didn't even know parents were expected to help, for example, with college—didn't know some did until I transferred to a university as a junior and learned it was common. I was used to finding jobs and working, making my own money. But I saw this as a unique circumstance. She was going to sell the Datsun, and it wasn't worth so much. I sincerely don't know why, but it strained me to ask. I was a father with two young sons, working construction, and I had sinful pride, but we could use a small break. That she hesitated caught me unexpectedly. It was that somebody else wanted to buy it from her. I told her I'd pay whatever the best offer was. Seemed fair, I meant it, so how could she say no to that? It was, after all, because she was now a widow with a shiny Eldorado, and a house I think was all mortgage free, and everything else, from him. And I'd pay her exactly the same amount as anybody would, right?

I didn't like it very much when she didn't sell it to me, though I didn't make a point of telling her. I also didn't like my brief flu of bitterness. Not shaking it off meant I wanted what I never felt offered, never really saw except as a pretense on a Christmas Eve or a birthday dinner over some overcooked hamburgers. What it confirmed was what I already believed from the beginning—it was the inheritance from my father I'd grown up with. So I came around to see her selling it to a boy across the street from her as the right ending. She wanted to help him out because he was going to UCLA soon, and he needed the car. And what he would do in return was drag out to the curb her one or two plastic trash cans every week. Because she did not like to do that. It was, probably, something my father'd always done. And from then on, it was this neighbor boy, every week, for many years too, which was particularly valuable as she herself got too frail, so it really worked out for her, I bet more than she could've expected.

I could never imagine growing up in a house with a man like my father, his culture, his world. Never, and never one moment wanted to. Could not for the life of me see how he and my mother would have survived two dates. But I am so grateful that he gave me a job when I was thirteen. That was it. It's who I am still, so I do think of him, and I do say thank you to him for that, even if it doesn't seem much like what you're supposed to be saying.

• • •

After I drunkenly crashed my marriage into a tree, there were several years of recovery time when I didn't know if I would receive, least of all deserve, the forgiveness of my sons. I wanted them to support their mom at whatever trade-off cost to me, and, willed by me and or slammed into me, I accepted its price. Though I clung to a hope, I feared I would forever lose not just the future with them, but that they'd tear up our memories like photos from a family album. The most happiness I had ever known were in these years of my life with my wife, my boys, us—our family, and my only family ever. I was so close to my sons. What I had loved about their mom more than all else about her was that from the moment of each of their births, I was less important to her than they were. Second place to one and to both. And that was not just right to me, but good, as in Right and Good, as in what nature commands instinctually. I too loved them, a love that fumbles around for words. More love, I would pronounce, than Abraham's, because I would have defied God's request to sacrifice Isaac if he were one of my boys. Again, I don't know how much that is my own psychic essence or is a consequence of my own childhood experience, if it is cultural or a creation, how specific or common. They were my favorite toys and pets and games, shows and sports, my best friends and my little brothers but best of all my sons. We watched TV when or if we wanted to, like sneaking, and threw tennis balls against the living room walls in the house to play keep-away, moving furniture to make space. Outdoors I hit baseballs to them and bounce-passed for them to drive to the hoop. I coached teams for nine years until I had to watch them from the stands. I bought them books they read and wouldn't ever and forced them into museums they yawned in, and their childhood was like having mine beside theirs and nothing whatever like I'd known at their age.

When my oldest son graduated from the University of Texas, his first job with his new bachelor's degree in journalism was a paid internship for a newspaper in Jackson, Tennessee. I was proud of him, of course, but I was thrilled like a girl getting her first date when he asked me to drive there with him for his move. And I played it cool like a girl on a date too. As soon as we were in his old Honda together, it was unavoidably more than only an adventure for me. Even though we happened to live near one another in Austin, where I was now employed, those were his college years, and, though worried all the time like any parent, I tried to let him have his father-free college years. Now the car seats were way too close together, and neither of us had traveled this kind of northeast to the South, and we had all the usual route conversations about maps and gas and road food. We tried to keep pace with the clutter of what seemed like the no speed limit of I-35, until we skirted the even more crazed Dallas traffic, and cruise-controlled I-30 and with all the trailers and rigs and satellite dishes and real thing country kitchens, passing the cities and streets that were Springs and Dales.

We sidetracked to Hope, Arkansas. I liked President Clinton. My son was obsessed with Bill Clinton like others might be Elvis. His birth home was much more modest than you could expect, even painted and cleaned up as it obviously was. With its new roof and new siding, it still wouldn't be one of the most desired houses in the definitely not rich neighborhood, since it was right against the railroad tracks too. And nobody but us was there to see it. My son wanted pictures and smiled like he'd found gold. Soon we were in Little Rock and did a repeat at the Arkansas State Capitol and then the Governor's mansion. We were alone there too. I took photos of him at the back gates, the ones where patrolmen were said to drive scandalous women in to visit our future president. My son laughed like he was thirteen again, but when I took the photo, he was back on board, his pose as adult as a cabinet appointment.

The Memphis Pyramid in sight, we crossed the Mississippi and not a few hours later we were in Jackson and eating at the restaurant of Carl Perkins, singer-songwriter of "Blue Suede Shoes," where I put it together that my son was a little nervous. I'd been nervous too, bitchy particularly along the way myself traveling I-40 about him driving with one hand and casually wanting to change lanes in front of tightly spaced caravans of gleaming eighteen-wheelers passing us like they were on the German autobahn. That is, in a foreign country. Which we were, which is where he was going to be living for a while. This was not like our homeland in El Paso, wouldn't seem to be Mexican or Chicano or a word like it and had never been. They even had gravy that was white. I remembered being his age—I'd never done or had the qualifications for anything close to this. I remembered how thrilled I was that he'd wanted me along. We visited his new job and we got a motel room and, when he wanted to go off alone, that seemed understandable. Probably it was my forehead that scrolled a *drive carefully!* message, because when he came back, apologizing for smashing into the back of a car at an odd intersection, it was as much him preemptively owning up to some shitty I told you so. No, I recanted, it happens, and to anyone, and no biggie if the other car was fine. No damage there, and the Honda lost some meaningless trim, and we got to shop for a new headlight at the Walmart and install that.

Realizing that it was through these incidents that you learn a town, it occurred to me that we should get a map. It was a small town, and why not see as much of it as we could before he started? Lay it out, learn a few streets so on assignments he'd feel less lost. He liked this as a practical idea, as a smart, educated guy, not as a son agreeing with a father. And that's when I had a moment: Like when he was born, my first, it was my own rite of passage, a move from one stage of life to another. Looking over the map, the big streets, the main drags, it was as though I was examining a metaphorical X-ray. No matter what I could guess, there was too much more I would never know as he would very soon. As to Jackson, we figured it was roughly five long north-souths and three long east-wests, and we drove them: Here's the industrial area, here's the poorest and Black, here's only rural, while this over here it's middle class mostly White, and up there's probably rich, all White, here's the old center, here's where all the chain stores are. It was a good day, and the next I was getting on a bus, leaving him there a grown young man, my son who I knew could take care of himself. How do you describe this saddest happiness of feeling your baby boy hug you goodbye as a grown man?

•••

Several years later it was a drive with my younger son, who had graduated from Stanford. We came out of El Paso and through the southern New Mexico desert, the mountain silhouettes of dead Indians, the mystical glyph of electrical poles, the train hauntingly silent at the near distance beside us, the peels of dead tires on the highway, the sky as blue as the best jewel. We bogged down in the construction that is the expanding Tucson and headed north at Phoenix, stopping for some luxury Thai noodles in the high-end theme shopping mall that is Sedona, and to stare into the stunning pit of the Grand Canyon until we finally took aim: This son was wanting to go to Los Angeles. He was wanting to see, taking notes and photos, where he lived his first three years and where I grew up too.

Where he was born there was only change for the better—the Silver

Lake area was even hipper than when we lived there, even if the weirdo On Club was gone—it'd been gone since before we left, transformed into a transvestite hang, and that was gone too. The Cuban coffee joint was still there, and Los Globos nightclub too. The duplex we rented from his conception to after his birth, the one overlooking Sunset Boulevard, was more tropically lush than when we were there, palm leaves shading the windows and doors. The cracks in the walkways of the apartment building in East Hollywood, where he lived next, were no longer where parsley was cultivated by the elderly Armenian couple, but the neutered ceramic boy in the dry fountain had passed the days like he was in Rome. We went to where I grew up, where Los Angeles Southwest College is now, on the land we called The Dips where I once found a dead body and knifed a boy, where the Río Theater was on Western. Drove him to the shopping mall on Crenshaw where that dumpy market now there was once called Food Giant and where that shabby drugstore really had the best scoops of ice cream. Showed him a bicycle route up Imperial that took us to the Watts Towers. We cruised over to Long Beach Boulevard, what is now almost completely little Sinaloa, and on Tweedy, the street that was for cruising just like Whittier Boulevard, we stopped for the best caldos de pollo and mariscos you could find on this side of the border—at least the biggest bowls.

It was time past in time now. Just the other day, a few years ago, in the past when my mother was young and too alive, wasn't dead, when I was younger than him, all this invisibly alive still in what is *me*. My son clicking photos, hearing the stories, seeing what I saw—this *seeing*, a mind-altering inhalation of father and son musks, actual or psychic, time gone and now, as much me as my memory of him is still as the smallest smiling baby, the memory not real and more than real, in a haze of symbol and myth, all the bright colors not yet faded to inevitable death, memory even when it's right there in front of you—in front of him. A son, precocious here too, who wants to know, who is taking notes to crack what is to all of us the source of this secret, the ontological paradox, we all have to live.

But here was a mystery that was revealed: I took him to that industrial laundry, the brick-veneered building my dad called the plant. Still so much as it was for me and I think my father too, not only memory. An old doorway, its old paint shedding, might be sealed and padlocked, a window near the large work table where all the prettiest women folded special orders, covered by plywood, but a business sign, painted in black and white on the red brick in the '40s or '50s, maybe the '30s, faded some, too high up, no reason to sandblast off. My son and I stopped and looked inside because the aluminum roll-up door was half open to let some of the hot air out, cooler outside air in. The laundry carts with wheels still around, the cloth bags of laundry now hung by hooks to automated, guided tracks on the ceiling that eliminated probably 90 percent of those long-ago jobs, likely including my dad's. We walked that same old cement sidewalk outside and came to the wide, open gate where the delivery trucks were parked and loaded. New trucks, new colors, new company name. There was a company-uniformed man standing in the yard by a truck backed into the loading dock. I started talking to him from a distance, going toward him, my son following. He was Mexican, in his thirties. In Spanish, I told him how my father used to be the floor boss, the super, for forty-nine years. I told him how when he worked here, when I worked here too, the truck drivers were always White guys, and the mexicanos were hidden inside. Everybody here's Mexican now, he laughed.

I looked inside the warehouse, and then back at my son. All they could do was kick us out. We went in. Through the stockroom of orders not yet in the trucks, the reserve racks of towels and linen, past that and up the ramp to the folding room, where I'd worked years until I didn't. I'd remembered it as you would your first bedroom, as huge, even if it was really the width of a closet.

Not a closet, it was at least half the size of what my memory preserved it as. Still big, spacious. And there were those mangles. The very ones, not replaced in all these years. They looked old when I was young. Seventy-five years? Since my first visits, they were the most impressive machines on the floor, steam wafting off their column-sized rollers. It was always so hard to explain what they were to anyone. To my son. Only now he was standing there, seeing what I'd seen since as far back as my memory could take me, even taking pictures. These were the machines that Felipa and María fed sheets forty hours and a half day on Saturday for double the years I'd been alive, each. There were three other mangles in the space, cooking the room more, raising the heat to at least twenty degrees more than whatever it was outside. One always had a line of women in front of a trough of napkins feeding damp towels. The others were pillowcases and tablecloths, all these items that had to be pressed and dried. And, from the other side, folded, and stacked, and bundled. More women on the other side, lots more women then. But that no more. Instead, it was a feeding machine, and in front of it, another machine that fed the feeding one. And behind, machines that took the still hot, ironed piece, another that folded it, and then, finally, a woman who put it on the stack.

Some things aren't understood well enough through words. Like most of the young in these United States now, my son had never been inside a factory. Intellectually, I knew that. But seeing that machine, operating, pushing out its hot, pressed product, was like . . . seeing that very machine. Knowing exactly what it was in its actual existence. So much that can be related can only be pointed to from a distance. An edge of it maybe, a corner. Its front. Like a memory, like a metaphor, the hope is that by glimpsing a part, a surface, the whole can be intuited. It just isn't always enough, and sometimes there has to be all of something, an entirety, to let through what time and space make impossible.

Maybe twenty-five feet from the door to the office, which would be the entrance and exit path to and from the time clock, hung a wooden-handled chain, painted black, that reached to whatever was way higher up above. That whistle was what made my father the most powerful man on the job. He pulled it in the morning, breaks, lunch, and longest, I'm pretty sure, for quitting time. Nothing I can remember him doing seemed to exercise more his job's authority and the pleasure that came with it. One time, I cannot even guess how old I might have been, he held me in the air. And I pulled it. This time we had was as close to that as I could offer my own son.

A LOS CIELOS DE MÉXICO

I am now officially phobic about sismos. I've been in three in Mexico City since this one.

I AM AMERICAN AND Mexican. Young, I had two points of view—both naïve, both proud—that laid out fifty-fifty. On the American side was the dream of sports stardom, its great fame and wealth, with wide boulevard smarts. On the Mexican side, there was the fantasy of Indigenous and mestizo defiance and ferocity, endurance and tenacity, alley smarts. As I got older, I took in the cynical racial truths of the American side, of poor people realities coming from across the border: It was a lot better to be born rich, and it was a lot better to find work where there was lush green that spread out and around, not a desert of rocks.

Neither side of me came with any background cash. My American father's was East LA poor, wage workers getting by. My Mexican mother's was culturally richer, even with stories that took a mythic family member—my *tía abuela*, a singer—to the presidential palace and then to Hollywood and led to my mom and *abuela* to LA—to work for minimum wage and just be another Mexican here.

I grew up on the American side with my single mother's beliefs and memories. And like most *mexicanos* who came across because they had to, there wasn't a lot of desire to go back. The refrain was that the government always thieved and cheated and lied, the church took too much away from the poor and used it to get power from the rich, there were no jobs and nothing much more than beans and dirt to eat and beer to drink. In the '70s, the Chicano movement that rose from young, newly educated Mexican Americans held out a more positive, romanticized vision. Not bad cops and drug scams, but a sacred, evolved Aztec past of high art, sophisticated agriculture, peaceful villages, gods of corn and sun and moon, princes and princesses dancing with feathers of quetzales.

Like every Chicano, I dreamed of traveling to motherland México, the *tierra materna*, to feel and know it myself. When we came out of our neighborhoods and into colleges, we met lots of others who'd been there. Often with their all-American families, they went to beach resorts and fishing villages, historic Indigenous sites, and shopped the coolest arts and crafts markets. Most of us, meanwhile, crossed to Tijuana, Juárez, Reynosa, Matamoros and bought the cheapest guitars. I used to joke—hey, *I've* been to Mexicali! We didn't get to make summer vacation decisions between Spain or Italy, México or Hawaii.

All Chicanos want to spend time in *la capital, la ciudad de México*. Mexico City was where the eagle landed on a nopal and ate a rattlesnake. The city of Moctezuma and Cuauhtémoc, of Cortés and Malinche, of la Virgen de Guadalupe, of the great pyramids of the Sun and the Moon, of Frida and Diego and Trotsky's death, the *museo* that holds the calendar of the Fifth Sun. And it was finally the years after my children had become adults that I could live there and get beyond the clichéd haunts and learn some of its actual life.

I sublet a *muy* nice apartment on the third floor of a seven-story building and was there in July. By *there* I mean in La Condesa, which is, along with La Roma, the younger of the two hippest colonias in the city. Where the bars and cafés are, where the nightlife goes till early morning; trumpets and sopranos are on the streets, art rules, and movie setups and modeling shoots take up large spaces in and around Parque México. Where there are more *bicicletas* than babies, more big dogs and little doggies than bicycles. Where there's not just chocolate and tacos al pastor, but sushi and shawarmas too. For me, who had already published books, it wasn't about the food or party. I was there to finally be a writer.

On September 8, 2017, an 8.1 earthquake centered off the coast of Oaxaca struck. It reached Mexico City, much of which is under an ancient lake, that lake especially under Condesa and Roma. The building swaying, I staggered down a marble staircase with no handrails and, like many, waited uncomfortably on the streets for what might be next. Devastating in the south, it was only scary where I was, six hours north. Of course there was more: Twelve days later, on September 19, a *sismo* of 7.1 hit closer, near Puebla. It struck more suddenly than the previous one, with intensity. The alarm sounded on the streets, but this time my building began rocking within seconds. I grabbed a bathroom doorframe and hung on for the ride. Things in the rooms behind and in front began falling, glass cracked and spilled, plaster dust clouded the air like snow and chunks of it fell from above and crumbled around me. The structural steel building pitched north south, east west. I could see the torque of it on the hinge side of the doorframe I clung to. I even had to clear my fingers when it seemed like the space between the door's edge and jamb were going to crush them. I watched for walls to fall. Until it was over. Thirty seconds? Forty-five? I don't know.

Blocks away from my *departamento* it was far worse. Buildings had collapsed that made international news photos. But video and still shots couldn't record the collective spirit that jumped out of every door. There was sadness and fear in everyone, but it slowed none. People, especially the young, rushed with bottles and jugs of water, shovels, pry bars, plastic buckets, food for emergency workers and for pets alike. Lines of people conveyed boulders of rubble. There were almost too many gathered who wanted to help.

I had come to México to be in its life, and here I was: Two fists raised signaled to all to be silent and still so rescuers could listen for survivors. Sometimes it was a hundred Brown fists, many dirty and sweaty, exclaiming to the heaven and all beneath. Done not as an anthem, not a symbol of fight or resolve, and though so near miraculous life and tragic death, not as a prayer. Stopped, hushed, it was only for listening harder, for going on and not giving up.

OILY HAIR CON SLICKED BACK NOTES ON GREASY LITERATURE

I love when pieces fall on your lap.

FOR A LITTLE OVER a week, I have been pulling at my hair over how to make this a fun piece to read. I mean, it can't be often these days that you get called a *greaser*. That's very *jajaja* and harharhar bicultural. It's particularly so when you consider it was tossed at *me*, a halfie who people usually guess Italian, Spanish, Greek—all of which the one who should have been my real father, Anthony Quinn, actually played on the movie screen. There was a time when I was into the look. Though not into using my Tres Flores as heavily as some of those old-school locos and zooters, I admit to strutting a wet, all-combed-back movida (there's even a book jacket photo of me así), and I would still tell you Tres Flores is good for your hair and that I recommend it, and not just because it's the cheapest. A mi me like it, that's it. I think dudes who are into it, ones out there on the street, I say it don't look bad—I say it looks *bad*. If that were my hairstyle now, would I then be somewhat guilty of not only perpetuating but reinforcing the stereotype? That said, however, so there's no mistaking the visual facts, when the below was transmitted about me, it was not my *peinado* being talked about, because I can tell you for sure that my current hair would have to be described as more hippie long than greased. It's not untrue that I will use, still, a palm smear's worth of my yellow oil to sort of add a little, I don't know, *luster*, or just that, *bueno*, a little *je ne sais quoi*, but the grooming complaints coming at me these days are more about length, not gloss. Or maybe I didn't wash my hair that particular day? I will confess this isn't impossible either. I don't like to wash my hair every day. It's that my theory is it's not good for hair. Okay, whatever, for *my* hair. So yeah, maybe it could have been more washed so those *muy limpios* could float and tangle in an outdoor breeze, so I, *al estilo* indie hip, could finger those away from my slacker eyes. But I would definitely take offense to anyone saying my hair was so dirty it looked greaser. No way. *Tu mamá, güey!*

Another aside before I get to what you will want to read below. Often I feel like I'm in some little known or understood country and I've been sent out as a scout. Not quite the same as someone in the military—my dad was a Marine scout in the Second World War and he would tell a story of reaching Japanese encampments where he'd get close enough to hear them talking and see them drinking sake. He and two men with him would have to dig holes to sleep unseen, and it was about that when I heard the worst rat story I've ever heard and have never gotten over it (rats as big as puppies burrowing against his warmth, and he couldn't scream about it or jump, nothing). I'd say I was more on an anthropological secret front, and I have to turn in occasional reports, and what I'm doing with this small piece is a preliminary report (the full story, which is me, isn't done yet). When I think this way, as I write this, I imagine Fox News attacks on me. See how that *greaser* is thinking about us, they will say. See how he's helping *plan* the *invasion*? No, not a Twilight Zone episode where the aliens are figuring how to spice good ole edible Americans. More like it's the '50s: He's a commie! they're calling me. Or, they're screaming that I'm communicating with all of them in Mexico! You know, like that. Yeah, I'm probably a well-trained paranoid, right? Still, I am prepared with a polite reply: Lighten up, man. I'm talking about literature here. But then maybe

I am difficult in a larger way too. I'm like, White people go to Mexico all the time, on vacation, or just cross the border to buy rum or tequila or a couple cases of cheap beer, and they come back and tell stories of Mexicans. Mexicans are this, Mexicans are that. I think, no, that was just an asshole. No, that was just a dummy. No, that was just a waiter being very polite. No, that was just some poor guy talking to an Americano tourist who is drunk and has money who is you.

I thus offer this emailed reaction to a reading I did in Virginia, at a well-known university, though the particular reading being discussed was at a side campus away from the major one, where I read the day before to a large audience. The generous professor who wanted me at the side campus had felt disappointed by the turnout, even as she had aggressively advertised, bannered outdoors, and stapled flyers indoors. The e, a student reaction, was sent to me because of its complimentary nature, innocently, to cheer me. For the record, I didn't care about how many were there. I was completely content by the turnout and never expected it to be as well attended as the enthusiastic professor did. Names (except mine) changed to protect the innocent.

> To those who missed out: On Thursday afternoon I walked
> into a classroom to hear Dagoberto Gilb share his work as an
> American writer. The only reason I felt initially skeptical about
> the session was that I had listened to Joe X speak at last year's
> Literary Festival and I was riveted, and I didn't think anyone
> could capture my attention in such a way again. X spoke
> about his work, but more importantly he spoke about his life
> through his work. The stage was wide and filled with flags and
> flowers. There were many people in the audience. At the center
> of the stage stood a huge podium fit for Dr. Y, our president. X
> had two or three colleagues give lengthy introductions. It was
> a big "to do" and rightfully so. He was as brilliant a speaker
> that day as much as he is revered as a writer. Dagoberto Gilb
> was no match for Mr. X. At least, that is what I thought when

I first sat down. There were no flags, no flowers, but on this day Gilb didn't need fanfare. He captivated the audience through his words alone. Although there were less than one hundred people in the audience, we all laughed, frowned, and cowered in harmony when Gilb read his stories. The Dagoberto Gilb Experience (DGE) was like being at a concert, sad movie, and a comedy club all at the same time.

When the audience had all taken their seats, Mr. Gilb was briefly introduced. Here was a greasy-haired, average-looking, seemingly personable guy standing with a handful of eight and a half- by eleven-inch paper. At first, I felt nervous for him. I didn't think this was going to go well for the speaker nor the audience. Gilb seemed to be just a little uneasy.

The first story that he shared was about a Hispanic boy growing up in Los Angeles. Gilb is obviously Hispanic, but spoke with an American twang. His tone completely took the role of the little Hispanic boy once he began to read. This reading was the movie part of the DGE. When he told the story it was like you were watching a movie about a boy growing up in a shitty neighborhood. Oh by the way, another part of the DGE is that he cussed. There was a wide variety of age groups and ethnicities in the room, but Gilb didn't seem to care that his work contained profanity because it was all part of the story. When Gilb was portraying a character from the story, he yelled out, 'Open the fucking door!' and the audience cowered. We were afraid for the boy. The man was angry at the boy's mother, but didn't mind taking it out on the kid. You could feel the pain in the room, and Gilb cracked a joke to cut through the tension. He picked up another pile of papers and began to read another story.

Please don't misunderstand what I am going to say—I was and am flattered. There was even more written, an equal number of words or more of more specific flattery. Who isn't vain enough to not feel empowered by words that are like a pretty woman flirting? (That last graph, there for the "obviously" line, also describes the opening pages of my novel, *The Flowers*. But that's not what I want read here. Which is: How often does one get to see the undergirdings, conscious and unconscious, of the How the System Works?)

Consider this text as a singular phenomenological document, as if the only evidence: Look at how writer X is described. Which is not at all. He is, in other words, normal. Whereas DG is Hispanic," and "average-looking" (Ask: What is he actually contrasting DG to, what expectation? And don't you wonder more, now, what X looks like?) and, in particular, "greasy-haired." When our reviewer came to X's reading, he was fully prepared for something powerful—if for no other reason than it was packaged thus. X had "colleagues," two to three of them no less, whose introductions were "lengthy," and the "to-do" was, as was the podium, big, "rightfully" fit for the president of the college. He was "brilliant" as a speaker and "revered" as a writer—proof of that simply the physical preparations there cited. He spoke about his life through his work (as if that were original, as if that weren't as much the markings of pomposity.) There were flags. There were flowers. Contrast to the expectation for DG (who was "seemingly" personable: Again, what contrast does that presuppose, what expectation?), for which so few came. No introduction by colleagues. No flags. No flowers either. No one, the reviewer thought, could capture his attention as well as X. He worried over DG. How could he compete with X? He had to be nervous, he was uneasy [aside: No I wasn't either], the audience wasn't up for it. And yet, YET, DG was good. Good despite it all.

It certainly will not come as much of a surprise that the above virtually defines the difference between a "mainstream" artist and writer and an "ethnic" one, defining expectations, dictating outcome, and, with time, quantifying returns (I mean income and status). Expectations coming in, expectations reflected out. It is not much different even today when, for instance, we might speak of one of the Latin American screenwriters or directors with the successful movies out in the last few years here, contrasting their fame with that of Americans. What's more peculiar here (and I mean this to transcend the extremely awkward conversation as it refers to me personally—my sincere intent), however, and more illuminating, is that both X and DG are American writers. Much of the difference between X and DG, in terms of credentials, is slight, as compared to the masses of lesser published writers below them. Yes, X has had a movie made of his (the question there, of course, is what comes first—couldn't the "revered" expectation going in from the start heighten the desire as a production is considered?) and, of course, that would account for the extra celebrity received. It seems an endless cycle that begins early and continuously gophers up squinting at many stages: It will certainly be pointed out, at the mature state of the writer's work negotiations, that X had 500 attendees, while DG had fewer than 100. And even if X were to have been credited with less than half of the "product" sales, maybe only 200, and even if say DG were to be credited for almost the most possible, say 80, it will thereby earn a shrug of no discussion when the time comes to divvy out the winnings from the free market.

THE HEXAGON OF THE CONQUEST

Rarely have I felt like I was a "real" writer. That is, one paid to write in measurable income. This piece was assigned by Harper's. I spent three weeks in Spain traveling, listening, and learning for this piece. Nothing but work pleasure. I really hoped it'd generate more gigs like it. I knew it was too long . . . but that wasn't why it never appeared in their pages. They were having a George Bush post-election obsession, then 9/11, and then the Iraq war, each a more timely matter. I still am proud of this not-in-our-time piece, even if it didn't alter the course of my writing career.

I DIDN'T LIKE BOOKS when I was young. Or, better said, I didn't play much with books and they didn't play much in my life. I played baseball and football and shot hoops when I could find them. I was good, one of the two who always picked sides on all elementary school teams. I lived in that dirty house in the neighborhood, the one where the yard wasn't mowed or edged, bushes overgrown, the neighborhood where I would learn, especially from other kids' parents, that *divorced* and *Mexican* were words that were dirty too and that kept me from having friends in neat houses. Then a new boy from another state moved in near enough when I was around twelve. My new friend wasn't athletic. He never talked about sports. I didn't care because at least I got to go over to his house, which was *the* dirtiest of them all, at the corner on a big street with a traffic light,

63

a house that was always for sale or rent. They rented. His mom looked like she drank, and his dad was a taxi driver. His dad, who was very quiet, sullen I'd put it now, lost his left arm working for the railroad. His dad could have been the one-armed man from *The Fugitive*! I never told my new friend how I smiled thinking it, not once, but it was always sort of *there*, making me feel like I was closer to a TV show world.

My new friend didn't even care about sports. He cared about what I had never heard anyone else talk about. If I wanted to go look at bicycles at a store, he'd go with me, blabbing about airplanes and space craft, flights to the moon and Mars. I liked Archie Comics, because of Veronica mostly, though *la güerita* Betty sometimes too, but he went for the superhero stories that were, well, too brainy and complicated for me. He knew dinosaur names and cared about science—he had both a microscope and telescope. He owned a few books, a used encyclopedia, and he knew about libraries too and he checked books out there. One time he walked me to his library, where I'd never been. It was a small local branch, with very few bookcases or books, though then it seemed otherwise to me, with big tables that we could sit in front of and spread out over. The library was a tense world to me, uncomfortable as maybe sitting for a meal at a family dinner table like people on TV shows did, as curious and unique to me as that. Different lightbulbs, air not from windows, only whispers and pages turning, and coughs, sneezes, and blowing noses. At first I looked at books he would show me with my eyes checking around me too, waiting for someone to criticize me for doing something wrong—I think now it was that strange feeling of time that really disoriented me, the hands on the clock moving either too fast or too slow. I looked, and I read with him, until suddenly I was initiated: I forgot where I was once I found a book on my own. We probably looked at it together, maybe or maybe not, because I only remember the book, which was about the Seven Wonders of the Ancient World.

Just think of them, or better said, the drawings of them in a children's book. The Pyramid at Giza, that obvious one of power, already as famous as the country of Egypt where there was the Sphinx too. The Hanging Gardens of Babylon was so much more to me because we heard in school so much about the Fertile Crescent, the rich dark land between the Tigris and Euphrates Rivers, where these walls and terraces held and nourished fruit and flowers that grew on them like ivy. There was Zeus in Olympus, a god-man made of gold, so big his head bumped the ceiling when he took this indoor throne. There was the Colossus of Rhodes on the Mediterranean, his feet planted on two land masses so that boats would have to go under him like a bridge. There were two in Turkey—the Temple of Artemis, who was the mother goddess of the wilderness, guarding the wild animals and nature, and the Tomb of Halicarnassus, which maybe was only another version of a pyramid, but to me was more a monument to death, the Big Grave.

That counts six. It's that I remembered number seven wrong. The correct number seven was the Lighthouse of Alexandria. Even now, to me, this one seems off. It wasn't as tall as Giza or the Colossus, it wasn't golden, it wasn't an attraction to all or most or certain beautiful birds of the western world—not one extra detail that would cause the imagination to dwell on its image or meaning. Bright as its light might be, important as I am sure it was for navigation, it was only practical. And so it was nothing like what I remembered, wrongly, as number seven, which was the Library of Alexandria. Could have been that these were so close, both with an "L of?" I was so sure that I couldn't believe it when I looked it up. But I say—*still* say—it has to be like number eight, no less than in the top ten! Doesn't it have to be? It was the library that collected all the knowledge combined of both the Greeks and the Egyptians, it held the library of Aristotle himself. That is, it was the symbol of knowledge, of its collection, of what a library is and does. And it was lost. Lost by Julius Caesar, the Roman conqueror, when he chased his rival Pompey and, in pursuing him, burned the Library of Alexandria down (accidentally, the story has it), and with it, or so it would seem, the oldest papyrus scrolls that were there, estimated to be somewhere between 400,000 to 700,000 of them. That's as though ancient history, knowledge, and wisdom itself were burned and it all had to start over.

• • •

I was in the state of Michoacán, México, ascending a mountain on a bus from Uruapan, and as the bus climbed we passed through clouds, as an airplane does, dark ones, a drizzle on the streets below them, and once the bus broke through there were lush, surreal green fields and fields of corn growing and then a village of *indigenas* living in stick shacks until, passing that, lower gear howling, came more cornfields and another village where furniture was carved and assembled and for sale and, climbing, more lush fields of corn until another Indian *pueblito* where bricks were made and sold, and then more *milpas* until, well, the bus leveled at what seemed a mountaintop, and I got off, in bright sunlight, at a *pueblo bonito* named Paracho, where the best guitars in all of México are made. One day later I was on a saggy horse as small as a donkey, a *burrito sin frijoles.* The toes of my boots barely hooked into the stirrups of the saddle and hung down like they might rut the dirt, while my knees were so propped up they seemed like they might poke the ears of my so-called *caballo*—I would have to have this saddle mounted over his butt to get the leg-reach I needed. My body complained that it was longer than a three-hour ride to the edge of the Parícutin volcano, through the avocado orchards that compete with California's, and since the horse— whose tired old *patas* had to carry my *huevos con frijoles*—also carried along my own gimpy left *pata*. I had a tearing Achilles and wasn't able to climb up to its gurgling, steamy mouth.

So I waited sitting on a big rock under a tree beneath it in the crunchy, grayish black *ceniza* that mulched the land below the wide horizon. I was there with Luis, the guide, who offered me some of his cookies, a cross between Marías and Oreos. Luis was a Purépecha Indian, a Tarascan, and told me, a *pocho* from *los estados*, that what they called him was a *mocho* because his Spanish, his second language, wasn't so good. He asked about the woman with my son and me—both of whom we could see practically crawling up the mountain on all fours through the sandy ash—if she were my wife. No, I said, we only met her down there, I'm single now. He slowly shook his head at me, surprised, even disapproving. Didn't I know it was bad for my health, he said, to not have a woman? His people marry when the woman is around sixteen, maybe fourteen, and the man is eighteen, or even sixteen, and stay married. The only reason to remarry is if a spouse dies. Nothing else is acceptable. Down there the people don't live as long as his people, who, with fifty years, he said, are at the halfway point of life. Luis was past calm, a blood pressure that could stabilize a hundred hearts in a hospital ward. Under his straw hat was a man I would have estimated to be between a rough-looking late forties or a youngish sixty. He was seventy-three, and not one fraying Achilles tendon.

Tossing the cookie wrapper to the wind, he stood up almost solemnly when I asked him to tell the story of the eruption. Before it happened there was a sign that crossed the sky, he said, a comet, but no one listened to that warning. Then one day they were working in the cornfields when the land opened and steam that smelled bad began coming out. It grew fast, within days, into a hill, and then just as fast the hill became a mountain. The lava came slow, not much at the beginning. The people crossed their arms with fear, afraid of what the darkness in the sky meant, and they prayed. At first they wouldn't leave. But as Parícutin kept growing, a big eruption came and the hot lava passed over the valley until—he pointed and named villages in the three directions we could see, the volcanic mountain at our back—the lava and ash were everywhere around here and over there, and everyone had to leave. Everything was lost, but the people who lived here only had to change their lives. And, Luis said, many now say the land is better.

• • •

After winning a vicious battle against the *indios* at the river they called the Tabasco after one of their own, what the Spanish renamed the Grijalva, Hernán Cortés devised a plan of peace. Through captured warriors he treated well, Cortés sent messages out offering peace to the Tabascan caciques, the village leaders. Meanwhile, he had his biggest cannon loaded with the biggest ball and told his men to fire it when he signaled. Next he had a mare who had just foaled be put together with a hungry stallion, then separated. He knew the *indigenas* were scared of this muscular animal they had never seen. When forty caciques came to talk to him in the afternoon, he told them, a little mad, that though he had many times offered peace, they had attacked and so it could be said they deserved to die. He explained that he himself was in the service of King Carlos, Emperor of Spain. It would be good if they were truthful in submitting to peace and his lord's, the emperor's, service, but if they were not, if there was a sense that they were going to deceive his king, then the *tepuzque*, the cannon they had experienced in their losing battle, would become angry. He secretly signaled for it to be fired, and it blasted and whistled. They were predictably terrified. He calmed them, saying he had given orders that they should come to no harm, and he called for the stallion to come near, next to Cortés and a tree where the mare had been and had left her scent. The stallion kicked, neighed, and stomped, his crazed nostrils making his eyes wild, staring right into those of the Tabascans. Cortés ordered the horse away, telling them that he told the horse to not be angry with them, since they came to make peace.

Afterward they ate bird and fish and fruit to celebrate their friendship, and the next morning the caciques brought offerings of ornaments—trinkets in the shapes of lizards and dogs and ducks, crowns and masks, soles for sandals, all of it a poor-quality gold. And Cortés was given twenty women, one of whom would forever be known as Malinche, who the Spanish called doña Marina, who spoke both Maya and Nahuatl. He asked them where they found their gold and jewels, and they told them it was in the direction of the sunset and that it was called *Culua* and *México*, words, places, and land he did not yet know.

When I think of Mexico, I imagine it like it could be a blurry memory, say if I were two years old, and I am being held on a dirt sidewalk, like an alley in El Paso, Texas, as Cortés and his column of men in suits of armor, sharpened swords and lances, high on horses that terrify me when I am beneath them, the ground-trembling clop of the hooves of those powerful legs prancing sideways, bells clanging on their harnesses, huge, mastiff-like dogs marching alongside, their tongues slapping between their long incisors, panting, all that ferocious animal heat and iron clang, as they approach an island city on a lake, the most beautiful they have ever seen, populated, bountiful, luxuriant, of fragrant trees and flowers and birds never seen in Europe, with tall buildings of stone and long, straight bridges, a terraced agriculture cut by canals and worked by canoes, a vision, a New World Venice, an enchanted land that makes the Spaniards feel they were dreaming.

Is there any story greater than that of the Conquest? Isn't the Spanish Conquest—less than fifty years from time of Cristóbal Colón, Hernán Cortés, Fernando de Magallanes, and Francisco Pizarro—the most fantastic tale in human history? It is *the* adventure story, a journey mythic and epic and evoking more the green blue red yellow black of primal exoticism, land and water and wind and sky, darkness and light, its subterranean jungle images and Homeric archetypes, emperors, kings, the gods with feathers and the God with a beard, savagery and nobility, sacrifice, cannibalism and gold lust, urges and acts both spent, wanton, honorable, deceitful, betrayals, lies, blood, semen, a story that would seem to brood and obsess more at a humid, fevered subconscious. It is *not* fabled sea monsters or a cliff at the end of a flat earth, but the factual account of the insemination of national histories that are now in the two continents birthed by it—and the transformation of the European isthmus that boomed not only through the plunder of Aztec, Maya, and Incan gold and silver and gems, but by a booming agricultural business—the fertile lands well-maintained by the *indios* became more productive of what Europeans already ate, while demand imported the new foods that came from there, like the tomato, the potato, corn, avocado, sweet potato, pineapple, coconut, peppers, squash, vanilla, and of course chocolate, and especially tobacco—all driven more efficiently by the massive import of African slaves and because of the unintended devastation of Indigenous cultures brought to submission not only by sword and cannon but by the conquerors' smallpox and measles.

The Conquest was the final human discovery event on the planet earth, the one after which any other human culture would have to learn that our natural world is on a globe, that it is defined, that here are its lands and seas: Any disagreement would simply be lesser knowledge. It was the last clash of huge, continental civilizations that did not yet even know of each other's existence.

...

The first time I was in Sevilla, Spain, I was in the center of the old city, any tourist's focus, when I found the entry in a dated, used guidebook I'd brought along: "The *Archivo de Indias*, the archive of the documents of the discovery and conquest of the New World, could be fascinating but little of importance is on display (old maps of Havana) and there's not a word of English." I was reading from the steps of the statue at the Plaza del Triunfo, which is between the great cathedral and its famous twelfth-century Moorish minaret—re-established as a Christian bell tower—known as the Giralda, the icon of the city, and another monument, the Alcázar, a tenth-century Moorish castle that grew in size and splendor to become the capital and residence of every Catholic monarch since Los Reyes Fernando and Isabel. Though on a map it was supposed to be visible from where I was sitting, I couldn't make it out, didn't think it possible that, if this were here, it didn't stand out not only visibly, but at least as flashing psychic klieg lights in a consciousness not just mine: It only gets a couple of sentences in this guidebook? Did I understand it right? Because if I did, if I was reading correctly, this archive, this library, kept all the documents of Las Indias, which in countries that are not Spain would be called Las Americas, what history calls the New World. In other words, the cultural geography after the Conquest, everything after October 12, 1492, the day a sailor from Sevilla, Rodrigo de Triana, among the miserable and mutinous crew only days before, yelled from high on the ship La Pinta, "*Tierra en vista!*" and Cristóbal Colón, with two other captains and a notary, rowed a dingy onto the Bahamian island he named San Salvador, sanctifying it in the name of the Christian God, claiming the land for Fernando and Isabel with the same royal flag of Castillo y León he'd seen less than a year before flying over the Alhambra in Granada, days after the final defeat of the Moors. It could mean that this library would possess the logs or itemized requisitions or receipts of the crew of Francisco de Magallanes—Ferdinand Magellan—on encountering the Mar Pacífico, which he named after he passed into the calm through what is now named the Magellan Strait at the tip of South America on his way to what would be called the Spice Islands, the land of cinnamon and clove, now the Philippines; it was the journey that ultimately proved that what was the European easternmost of the East Indies could be reached by traveling the waters west. It would surely mean that it would own the pleas written by Hernán Cortés to His Majesty, arguing for his honorific place as Governor of Mexico. It might also have correspondence documenting the smallest details from Cajamarca, Peru, after the ruling Inca, Atahualpa, drawing a line above his head inside the building where he was prisoner, believing he would negotiate his release, offered to fill the room to the height of his reach with the gold Francisco Pizarro and these Spanish craved so much.

I walked around the small area in Sevilla's center until I got spun around and then wasn't sure which direction it would be relative to the map and so I asked someone. Right where I was standing. It was the building with the huge stone nautical pilings and heavy anchor chains surrounding it. I found the glass front doors all by myself. The Archivo was closed, a uniformed guard said, and there was nothing to see for now. Can I just look inside for a second? He allowed me, trusting me, but watching. Maybe it was the marble stairs that would take me up for a peek at the closed doors above them, but my feet felt so tiny, and the stairs so big, and the silence came at me as wide and distant as clumsy childhood fear and awe.

The Egyptian Library of Alexandria is lost forever, but right in the heart of Sevilla—which for two hundred years, as the capital of the Conquest, was the richest city in the world for not only the Indigenous gold and silver that would cargo up the Río Guadalquivir, but as the port city of all trade coming into and out of the New World—there is a library archive that has amassed all the documents of trade, law, and government from the last great political, cultural upheaval in our human history. If there were an interest in an updated, color-drawing book of a current, surviving Ancient Wonders of the World, and if, as I believe, it included a library holding our most valued ancestral documents, then it would surely feature the Archivo General de Indias.

...

I have returned, determined this time, to touch the wonder, to report on the mystery. At the Barcelona airport, after a flight from London, I am in the middle of the customs line about to pass through a glass door to the kiosk. I do notice the slobby dude—in baggy pants and an oversized long-sleeve sports team shirt and some neck bling, which swings from side to side, I think a Latino if there is such a thing in Britain—cruising up to the front, his shorter, thin, comparably dressed but more embarrassed partner at his back. Way behind I hear that fierce and raspy *española* voice. Though it has to be some, it's not just cigarettes. She starts in Spanish but switches into a good-enough English, telling him that there is a queue, and we are all in a queue, and he needs to step back into it like everybody. He ignores her, shoulders bobbing and pressing forward, when here she comes into his face, telling him right up into it. Don't touch me, he says, his first words. She says how maybe in his country he can get away with this, but not in hers. He says how it is his country, his a more under-his-breath reply. She steps in front of him, her arm out and palm up in his chest, trying to hold him back, definitely slowing him down. She says, for anyone to hear, that she is calling a security officer. He says how he is a security officer. She says, louder, she too is a security officer. All this in English. I don't think the dude or his cuzz spoke Spanish. I pass them by and get stamped through. I am officially here, even if I have one last flight.

The next day, a Friday, I've awakened in Sevilla, and nervously I'm on my way toward my destination, the sky as blue as the Yucatán's, admiring the Barrio Santa Cruz, the maze-like, pre-Inquisition Jewish neighborhood, clearly the city's most picturesque, which shares walls with the Royal Alcázar, what many who'd never seen Spain would think of as, say, so Mexican if they were in Xico or San Miguel de Allende, where my gimpy foot and I get turned around. Redirected, and through a couple of plazas shaded with *árboles de naranjas*—orange trees—the Arabs introduced to the Andalucia region, on cobblestones and on mosaic sidewalks intricately patterned with tiny stones individually set on their edge, I enter a tunnel that, punching through, frames the Giralda—a photo every single Japanese tourist in every group snaps. Not a hundred paces west, past the massive wooden front gates of the Alcázar, I slip under the giant chain and move along the side of the Archivo de Indias to reach its public entrance. The building itself is the sixteenth-century former Casa Lonja de Mercadores, created to stop all the nasty stock market–like business taking place at the steps and inside the cathedral at the peak of the era. But where I need to go, I am told, is a building across a small cobbled street with more glass doors and a Ministerio de Cultura sign above it. Guards direct me through a metal detector, I check my work bag, and limp up more stairs. I have a letter to allow me in as an *investigador*, a researcher, I have a passport, I have two official photos. I answer questions typed into a computer application. Not Mexico, I say three times, I'm from the United States. I fill out multi-duplicate forms of names, numbers, and dates about where I am from, staying, representing, researching, and then I am given, besides a rules and information sheet, green and pink in blue stencil *ejemplares* of what I have signed and a photo ID *tarjeta nacional* with my own number, signed and rubber-stamped on both sides. The pages from my yellow legal pad have to be torn in half, and they all have to be loose. I can only carry and use a pencil. Laptops are allowed.

I am introduced to skinny and voluble José Antonio who tells me how unusual it is that I would get to see the archives themselves. I have to see them, I explain, because that's why I'm here. It's not a particular few documents I am interested in. It's that I have to see the whole of them. How they're stored, how high stacked, how deep the aisles, how unlit the space. It's the archive, the library, that's what I'm wanting to learn about. I want, I tell him, to think of it as the Ancient Library of Alexandria. I can't tell him how the more I imagine it, the more it becomes a Hieronymus Bosch painting in my mind, a medieval space so vast that people shrink, and then these pale, small people scurry around, ancient scrolls in both arms. Or maybe a Gothic German painting, a stooped old man at the top of an old, old, tall wood ladder, his thick wire glasses dangling from his nose and ears, and he's squinting, reaching into a faraway corner. José Antonio says it's not usual to be taken to the *depósitos*, it's not normal, it's not done, but wanting to be generous, he will ask the assistant director tomorrow, he will see what she says, he will tell me what her decision is.

On the way to the *sala de investigadores*, I apologize to José Antonio for my slow movement. It's that I have a *pata mala*, I tell him. He shakes his head. *Pierna*, he corrects me, or *pie*. Only animals, he says, have a *pata. Y por eso*, I say, they tell me I have a *pata*. Where I'm from, I'm considered an animal. He stares at me, shrugs, but I can't make sure he knows I'm joking around because, too late, we are in the guarded research room. It is several aisles of shoved-together tables, four computers per side, around fifty seats total, and only a few empty. Many, many serious-minded people are busy in the silence. He gives me what seems like a giveaway pamphlet about the archive as I sit, and then shows me how to use the search application in the computer, the archives' category list, a computer version of a card catalog but with a few extra features. For example, in moments, I am staring at a digitized copy of a letter from Cortés. And José Antonio goes back to his own work, and I'm alone feeling really ignorant. Really dumb. Like a horse, or worse. I have no idea what I am going to do here. I don't even know enough history, colonial or pre- or post- or otherwise except for a few books, to ask specific questions. I'm like, I heard about Babe Ruth and Mickey Mantle and I'm sitting in the room with every baseball card ever created and I only really know the name of a few teams and virtually nothing else but home runs. And it's a PC machine and I only know Macs. I keep messing up what the effect the right versus the left click has on the application's functioning and split screen—you hit this link and a description of what's in it pops up over here—and I can't make any of it do what I think I might want if I have any of it right anyway.

When I get up the courage to try the man at the reference desk, José Antonio's compadre Javier, he comes over. He's got the expert look of years of conscientious employment here. What do I want? he asks rhetorically. Say I want this, he answers. Click.

Then click. Then click here, *vale?* Want to see this? *Vale*, click. Click click click. *Vale?* And he goes through it again. *Así, vale?* He does this all so fast, so skilled. Easy, his pat on my shoulder says, going away. Could I say, *bueno*, well, *es que*, maybe if after each of those clicks you paused, *bueno*, ten to thirty seconds and, *bueno*, I stared and, wait, stared at the screen before the next click? And then you went through it, oh, like ten more times and explained every single thing and the history behind each?

Sad, defeated, I decide to make my first day one that's out of there early. As I hobble onward, the guard at the exit is on a walkie-talkie, eyeing me. He asks my name. My name?

He writes it on a clipboarded form. Looking up, he tells me I have a *folleto* belonging to the Archivo and I need to return it. This? It looked free to me. I walk it back upstairs, embarrassed. *Vale*, now they know I am here. Outside, I am ashamed. *Bueno, pues*, I am a gimp. I am resigned to giving up my NBA career. I know I will definitely have to say no to the mile-relay Olympic team if I'm asked. But *this* too? I can't even read what I don't know anything about anyway. I can't click a computer mouse without wanting to throw it across the room or smash it like a Texas roach. Quietly though, no screaming, real quietly I swear, no breaking any noise rules. It's that I wasn't expecting computers or software issues at the Library of Alexandria.

Not to slump and limp too mopey and lose the whole day, I drag the achy foot across the street to the public entrance to see the public display of the Archivo de Indias. Maybe I should have started there in the first place. Maybe I should know *something*. At the outside stairs, a male voice catches me from behind, telling me how he's working on material from a seventeenth-century political murder in Mexico. He even invites me to a goodbye party for one of the *archivistas*. Yes, I gimp, and therefore I am a gimp, but I just got me a party on my first night! And so I lift both *pie* and *pata* up those marble stairs that are not so intimidating now that I have not only a party to attend but an official government-issue ID, like a membership card.

The public space of the Archivo offers a spacious, if dark, gallery of regally framed, official portraits of uniformed men, and the expansive marble floors and arched ceilings are circled by faux bookcases of empty *legajos*, designer quality boxes decorated by engraver's ink, where actual documents could be stored. Somewhere deep within this building there are real, filled *legajos* like these, and there are employees—little people scurrying in a cool, dimly lit basement, somewhere nearby—moving them up and down and sideways: There are around 43,000 *legajos*, and somewhere close to eighty million pages, three centuries of documents with details and implications small and large, historical, economic, political, social, religious, engineering, architectural, cartographical, concerning the southern United States, Mexico, Central and South America to Tierra del Fuego and east to the Philippines, and the Spanish government has set in motion a plan to digitally scan them all and has scanned approximately 14 percent of them. As my eyes stare glassy into display-case examples of early sixteenth-century escudos—royal coats of arms designed for newly anointed nobles, some even related to Indigenous royalty—I am wondering how many people it took and how much so far to get to that percent, and (this is how I am) I am visualizing these ancient pages rolling through a scanner that resembles a mechanized tortilla-maker, that last step a drop onto a dark *manito* that makes a neat, counted stack. Alone with the vast breadth and width of elegant physical space and my imagination, suddenly I see a couple who look like my own territorial descent, and then I hear them whispering in English. I can't keep myself from asking. They are a Mexican American couple from Los Angeles, and the one who is a professor says she saw an entry in a guidebook, and, like me, she had to know if it was for real, she had to go inside: I am in Spain, they have taken my name down, and, *¡ajúa!*, my brain is not alone in its peregrinations. It isn't only me who is eager to see into the cultural and historical looking glass that we didn't even know existed.

• • •

I worked in a library for a few years when I was in college. Although there are passers-through, those who visit for their needs and go, it's the ones whose lives are in them who are the special stories. Let me give an example of what I mean. I had a boss who was this huge man, at least six-five,

275 pounds, maybe more. Big as he was, though, he didn't seem big, because he was all feet and shoes, like he was still growing into them, and maybe also because everything about him seemed as soft as his voice. He was as kind, caring, and gentle as St. Francis, which made sense because, before he became a librarian, he'd been a Franciscan priest. He knew Latin, to speak it too. To me, that meant he lived in a Pure Other World I could only imagine as might a pre-teen boy getting hormones, squirming with awe and fear on the idea of a voluptuous, naked woman. Then one day he fell in love. If I were a *viejita*, this would have been a fanning-myself *susto*, because, to me, he was still a priest. He fell in love with a woman who was very big. He loved her so much he bought her flowers all the time, excessively. He bought her chocolates, boxes of the best chocolates, excessively. And they must have eaten them together because they both got bigger and bigger. Then they, together, decided to lose weight. Following weight-loss books precisely, they did. And then, just as suddenly, just as body and soul mysteriously to a young me, he became huge again. I can't remember if she left him or if that had nothing to do with it. His clothes changed, he forgot to shave, his hair wasn't just unruly but scissored unworldly, not for style or as statement. It was said, quietly in the library of course, he was drinking too much. I'm not sure which made this story a story I remember, whether it was that he was a librarian or a priest. It is only one of them. But it reminds me of going to the library.

With my *investigador* card, laptop, and my pencil, I have begun a routine of mornings of going there. I receive a familiar castellano *bueno día*—s's dropped—from the men in uniform as I clear the screening machine. I give my bag to the kind lady at the desk, hang the coat, and gimp upward. As I pass through the glass door of the *sala*, a silent mutual nod to that guard, I hand my card to the non-reference-desk employees directly responsible for physically keeping track of both the *legajos* and researchers. I am given a desk number where I sit.

Before I traveled to Spain, thinking on paper, I'd made a first list of topics that I could look to find paragraphs about. They were very naïve and not very historical, I knew seconds after I became more expert with the clicks. I hereby disclose them publicly: food on ships, wages, chocolate, *los escándolos, los secretos, las atrocidades*, sex, moving and storing gold, smoking tobacco, dogs, ask what has been stolen from the Archivo. Those as though the Archivo would be some encyclopedia, not a document library.

Still limited by my own broad—and only broad—knowledge of the Conquest and its conquerors, I'm clicking better and narrowing down names and places, for example: *Cipango, Cíbola, Padre Francisco de Bobadilla, Cuauhtémoc, Malinche, Bartolomé de las Casas, Juan de Cartagena, Manco, Atahualpa, Francisco de Carvajal, Diego de Orellano, Tzintzuntzan, Pátzcuaro.* I've also started letting my nosy eyes go around the room, this research room, to these people in the library who have a computer and a pile of almost ancient paper near that. A few I met at the party I went to, which, like Sevilla at the time of the conquistadores, was attended by an international array of people—Canadians and Americans and Spaniards, *italianos, alemanes, franceses, flamencos* (Flemish was what King Carlos I was too, and because of his royal court, the word in Spain came to describe anything "flashy," like the traditional dance most recognize as its only meaning)—plus a few more I look to give little waves to: a Sri Lankan *bella* being paid by a company to find everything she can on *cacao*, a New Mexican finishing an art history PhD about mirrors in Cuzco, a *madrileña* researching Tierra del Fuego, an Ohio historian on eighteenth-century Peru, a *chilango* studying *los mayas*, a Texan the seventeenth-century New World book trade, a *sevillano* Puerto Rico, a Tennessean the slave trade, a Parisian researching Nueva España, a Florida historian amassing material for a book on Nueva Granada.

It's always the usual sneezes and sniffles and nose-blowing that percolate the silence, the strolling guard monitoring the room like it's a bank. The other Spaniards, employees and not, both the men and women, can be spotted by the almost Catholic school consistency of clothes—a striped cotton dress shirt, collar out from under a dark pullover sweater. It's that I like to know how it is within a workplace—and what's *down there*. And *he* went there every day, I was sure of it. He being this very stern, small, older man who rolled the institutional gray cart in and out and down and up the elevator when requests came to see pages in a *legajo*. Unlike the stereotype of the Spanish male, of the balding dome and thick, farsighted glasses, his mixed black and gray hair was all there, and his glasses were for myopia. But he also had an odd white patch of hair, like a bandage, at the back of his head. He did not talk to the others much, and if some non-employee incidentally spoke to him, he sighed like he was clearly indisposed and above such verbal interfaces. He was my evidence, he made it more curious. What was it like down there? I politely ask José Antonio if I have been given that permission yet. The one who gives this, the *directora*, he explains, is not here, maybe tomorrow. He will find out, he will try. He didn't have to say each time how unusual, how not normal.

At my assigned desk, I am at the Archivo computer, and this is the beginning of the large topic catalog list:

PATRONATO (Foundation) 1480–1801
CONTADURIA (Accounting) 1514–1782
GOBIERNO (Government) 1492–1870
JUSTICIA (Justice) 1515–1617
CONTRATACIÓN (Trade) 1492–1795
ESCRIBIANA (Court Records)
ARRIBADAS (Arrivals)
CORREOS (Letters) 1752–

Hit any of these, and more links rain beneath. Hit those, more. And so on. Or go to a small window, type in a name or a place or a phrase, wait, and a list of hits unfurls. Yes, I was told, it probably takes at least two weeks of—and I quote an eloquent and sophisticated American—"spazzing around" to get any idea of what's going on. As I am beginning my battle with my own daily twitches, typing in "*plata en Charcas*," because of the story of a local in Potosí, who, chasing a llama up a hill and, climbing, pulled a weed and found silver pellets on its roots, thus originating the richest silver mine ever known—when—this I swear—in walks a new guy, who is even seated right across from me. He has the quiet, utterly polite, dark face of an *indigena*. He has that first-day look of fright and intimidation as he is awaiting the click click instructions of Javier. He moves eyes that do not intrude, do not look straight at, that angle down. In the *sala*, as you are never supposed to share physical material, you are also not supposed to share talk material either. A rebel, I lean forward and whisper. He's from Bolivia. He's a *religioso*, and he is studying *los dominicos* (the Dominican Order) in Charcas.

I want to pull paper and find silver. I want to discover something, the library search version, I want time to disappear. I consider several subjects. One about livestock and "also about the condition of those *indios*." Another on how Admiral Colón discovered Panamá. Another on Juan de Oñate and New Mexico. Another on doña Marina and her service to the country. Ones on the population of Perú after the conquest, on Cortés's complaints to the king, on the registration of slaves.

Many of these you can see digitally. All you do is select *ver imagen* (see the image) and on a screen there it is (even through the web—www. aer.es), e.g., the Papal Bull and Treaty of Tordesillas, which drew the latitudinal line through South America, making everything east of it Portuguese territory, like Brazil, and the rest conveniently belonging to Spain. But I had to actually see and touch the ancient paper. I had to find something that would allow me to click the *solicitar fondo* link, which causes the man with the square white patch of hair to descend.

I decide to click on Fernando (or Hernando) de Magallanes. In a paragraph, here's why his story is so especially fascinating: Magellan leaves from Sevilla in August of 1519 to find the western route to the Spice Islands, the East Indies. He loses one ship on the coast of Brazil and fights back a mutiny. As he strains for five miserable weeks around the tip of South America, he loses yet another ship when it deserts him and returns to Spain. When he finally passes out of the strait that will be named after him, the breakthrough is into such calm that he names the ocean *el pacífico*. He comes onto the Islands of Saint Lazarus, what later we will know as the Philippines. He supports an island king of Sebu whom he has converted from Islam to Christianity. Fighting on behalf of this king, he is killed in a losing battle. Disillusioned, the king massacres all but two of Magellan's twenty-nine officers. In all, 115 men escape the island. Months pass, more crew die. Another ship is burned. The two that remain finally set sail and even find the East Indian islands of the Molucca that were the original goal, where they load their ships with cloves, nutmeg, cinnamon, and they begin their return journey to Spain. The *Trinidad* springs a leak, and eventually only four survive starvation and disease. The *Victoria*, captained by Sebastián del Cano, rounds the African cape and, in September of 1522, makes it up the Río Guadalquivir to Sevilla with its spice cargo and eighteen men, the first to ever circle the earth.

I don't wait long for my request to ascend on the gray cart. When the package is passed to me, I feel magic and mystery. I give a pause of deep respect as its weight is hefted to my timebound hands and I carry it to the table. A *legajo* is secured by one long, white cotton ribbon—everyone must learn to wrap and tie a *legajo* just right, be professional. The design of its cover is classic highbrow European: the lettering, an old typeface in caps, *Archivo General de Indias, Sevilla*, and artwork, a linocut etching of, in the foreground, soft naked boys dumping their bounty of fruit and bread from baskets, behind them a king probably, with two archbishops or cardinals on either side of him. The box unfolds on all four sides, revealing the document inside, which also has a tie.

I do not believe what I have has been looked at much, if at all. When I turn a page—bound by a string binding—there is that clinging together with another that new books as we know them have when pages haven't been turned. The aged cream paper itself is thick but soft. Created from a wood paste, if looked at carefully, there are even little bluish lines in them for a pen to follow. These pages have survived a fire, because the edges, particularly on the bottom, have jagged dark brown and black burn lines. There is about an inch-and-a-half hole that almost looks like it has been punched out and then put back perfectly. I fear touching it. The all of it is, from the found art point of view, terribly, startlingly beautiful. I turn pages as though each is an unframed canvas, a fragile tissue. I cannot imagine getting used to them. I cannot imagine that anyone is letting me, for example, touch them.

Inside are supposed to be descriptions of payments made to these men on the ships, both survivors and dead, what the cargo was, how money was divvied up. And yes, I can see a list of names and numbers. The names, yes, I can even make out, to some degree. But I really cannot read any of it, not really. I cannot read anything in this *legajo*, and I probably can't read the vast majority that would be dated before at least 1700. There would be, of course, always the issue of language when studying one that isn't what you primarily speak or read. And then it wouldn't be only that it is in Spanish, but that it's in a Spanish that is an older idiom, much older version at that, with words and phrases that are out of common use.

And then there's the issue of abbreviations, recording shortcuts, that have to be learned: Trying to read these texts not only as a non-expert, but then to read as one would a court reporter's shorthand. And then, finally, there is the penmanship itself. Reading anyone else's writing is often an eyestrain. That, however, would not be the trouble here. Because the documents were almost always written by human typewriters, *escribanos*, whose calligraphy skills were equal to and as important as carpenters on ships.

The sum of it is this: When I look at any of the pages, I am looking at an artistic rendering of letters and words and sentences—the margins, for example, all around are filled in by swirls that look like infinity marks with yet an extra dimensional loop of emphasis, or swirls that are tight, dark tornadoes or loose, weak springs, or worms, or curls, or curlicues—every garnish and flair that is possible. The first letter in a sentence is not just a cap, it's dressed in the finest feathers and hat and shoes and gloves. If it's the first letter of a paragraph? The letter swoops off the sides of the page and swings up and over into empty space. You can only admire what happens within a text to an *e* or *f* or *m* or *p* or *z*, just to name a popular few.

At a distance, the script could seem like ancient Greek, or Coptic, or Aramaic, even Arabic, maybe Egyptian, a language that might have been in Alexandria. Hieroglyphics. On the page, it is an ancient, unknown script that has to be learned, must be taught by someone who already knows, like through an initiation. Or through what is scientifically named paleography. I was told by a professor working in the Archivo that this is exactly one of his courses. After a few months, he told me, depending on a mastery in Spanish, pages written by a conquistador, one maybe some years after Colón, can begin to be deciphered. After six months, a person can begin studying *pleitos*, legal arguments, about encomiendas, salaries, or royal titles. As to him, in his lifetime he will never be able to read all the material there is in his own area, even if it were all he did. Which is a lot like me, because I know I can never read all that I wish to either, except for me, a gimp, I cannot read any of it.

Inches near an actual document, I am still so far away. From then. From time. From seeing clearly the colors and lines that might make sharper images in my mind. And if I *could* read any word, most, every word even, how much closer would I be then? How much less a dream, how much still like a "memory" that is as accurate as a two-year-old's, even a precocious one's? How near must I get to be fulfilled? With what kind of eyes or seeing glass? What quantity of books, or detail from one, in a library, in an archive, will finally get me there, wherever it is I want to go, whatever it is I want to learn?

• • •

I step, I drag, I step, I drag. Well after two in the morning, the streets of Sevilla tap many melodies of shoe heels walking fast, walking slow. Voices, single and in groups, echo loud, singing, laughing. Three Spaniards, dark leather coats and neck scarves swung over the shoulder, drunk and happy, bump up to me, asking directions. When I tell them how I wouldn't know and where I'm from, they squeal—one's been to Houston, one's been to El Paso! The cobble streets are wet from being washed, and the cool black air around the plazas near the Giralda, the Alcázar, and the Archivo stirs the sour of burning cigarettes and the sweet of fresh horseshit from the tourist carriages. In *el centro* of Sevilla, the quietest hours come at dawn and a few after. Nothing really opens before 10:00 a.m. or later.

On my way to Mérida earlier than that, above the cooler shadows of the narrow streets in Barrio Santa Cruz, high-definition sunlight sharpens the tone of the whites and yellows of walls and the reds, greens, and blacks of higher-up, flower draped, wrought-iron window terraces. I am saying to a taxi driver how a walk to the bus depot would be nothing without my *pata mala*. He asks me if I know the difference between *pata mala* and *mala pata*. I laugh and I say that if my bad foot is bad luck for me, it at least makes good fortune for him. The word *fortune* makes me tell him about the pretty, flirty *gitana* in Córdoba who, on my last little side trip, momentarily played my vanity and my discouraging, unhandsome gimp into a stop, offering me dried sage and insights into my future after she called, *Por favor, guapo*. Says the *taxista*, we don't have gypsies here, only *romani*.

I am on my way to Medellín, a few kilometers east of Mérida, which by bus is three hours north of Sevilla, because I want to see the *pueblo* where Hernán Cortés was born. Always when I've read stories of the Conquest there are these remarks about Extremadura, the region where so many of the men had come from, especially Cortés and Pizarro, whose hometown of Trujillo is a few more kilometers east of Medellín. In histories, this land is always described as hard and barren as its name, and that this explained why men from there were so hungry and brutal, why they were so successful at their occupation. If Andalucía, the southern region where Sevilla is located, is the land with the film resemblance to the Old American West in spaghetti westerns, then Extremadura must be the almost uninhabitable desert from Juárez to Chihuahua, or New Mexico's parched *jornada del muerto* trail region that goes north from Las Cruces.

Maybe once it was barren. Maybe. I doubt it. From the bus windows it looks plowed and planted, a cross between the cotton and green chile fields that grow well in the upper and lower Río Grande valleys of El Paso and southern New Mexico. There are patches of land where fields of rocks, even boulders, begin to share the ground with what seem to be hardwood trees, like live oaks, and when I see what seem like limestone breaks, and groutless but carefully fitted stone fences, and nopal cactus and horses, and cattle, then it seems it could be what south of Austin is called the Hill Country, one of the most naturally beautiful and, if rugged, lush parts of the state.

I arrive in Mérida too late to catch the morning bus to Medellín, and I have several hours before the next one goes there in the afternoon, a man at the depot office tells me. A man next to him figures out what it is I'm doing, because he'd been to México. *Todos los conquistadores son de aquí*, he tells me. *Las mierdas se robaron la plata de todos*. (All the conquistadors are from here. The shits stole money from everybody.) Pizarro, he singles out as his personally favorite example, came from a family that raised pigs only a few kilometers from here. My driver is the *gerente*, manager, of the depot and, since he has to drive there anyway, offers to drop me off downtown. "The rocks right here," he says, pointing to a wall of them after we cross a bridge over the Río Guadiana, "to them, when they were in the Yucatán, reminded them of these rocks, so they named it Mérida there too." He leaves me at the Teatro Romano, which is to say, the site of the Roman Theater, built in the teens of the first century by the son-in-law of the Roman Emperor Octavian Augustus. Not too far from the theater is a first-century amphitheater, one of those rings for gladiator versus animal events. Across the street from the Roman Theater, a very contemporary Museum of Roman Art displays much of the public sculpture of gods and goddesses once worshipped in the city. Also of the emperor himself, if for no other reason than the city's name descends from being named in honor of him, Emérita Augusta. It was the capital city of one of Rome's most important regions, Lusitania, known for its marble and wood and grain crops, its most eastern port (it included what is now Portugal), a stopping point for trade and travel from the east, north, and south on the peninsula. Gimping toward the river to get back to the depot, through this photo-shoot beautiful city, I pass by the Roman Templo de Diana (the Greek goddess Artemis), the emperor's cult, the goddess of the hunt, of the wilderness, around twenty granite columns that stand twenty-five feet high, until, walking more, I reach the cut-boulder walls of a major Moorish castle that goes to the river's edge, where it overlooks Rome's longest and best surviving bridge.

Not a half hour after I've crossed *el puente romano*, the Roman bridge, I have made it onto a commuter bus of old people and teenagers that has a stop in Medellín. It crosses more plowed and budding fields and prickly pear and rocks and towns painted as bright as any nurse's uniform, the towers and steeples as Arabic as they are Spanish. Getting closer, as we pass some groves, a *viejo*, very kind, with those glasses and beret covering the balding dome, tells me how they are *nueces* (walnuts) on this side, and *peras* (pears) on that one. Fences hold bulls, horses, sheep. Medellín is a white-washed *pueblo* set up against a river and a prominent, almost God-above rise of a green hill which is crowned by a castle, a massive tenth-century Moorish fortress of brown stone. Even if this picturesque village of now was a tenth its size then, *this* was there. When I stop at the café-bar Palomares in the center of the city, waiting for the return bus, a *cerveza* and *media ración* of deer meat, all I am able to think of is the history of the Romans down the road, and the boy Hernandito prancing up the hill, bouncing his rubber ball against castle walls. Like my new best friend long ago, he probably imagined superheroes, and instead of sports and their leagues, he had gigantic, mythic trophies of conquering and conquered empires all around him.

· · ·

I had to get back to Sevilla quickly because my time was running out and I still hadn't been *down there*. Days before, I had nagged good-natured José Antonio enough times until finally, one day, there was a shift in the discussion. I needed a document to give *la directora* to approve. He suggested a letter expressing my purpose. He suggested I write it on the spot, on my laptop, and he'd print it for me. Everything, of course, had to be documented. There was evidence of this want and need functioning everywhere around me. I felt like someone from so many of these archived pages entreating Her Royal Majesty the Queen. And so I composed. I felt it was essential to craft well my request, but also with speed and a confidence in my command of reasoning and word, yet displaying my determination. I believe I achieved this. Thus it was printed out, and it was passed forward and up and onward. A stamped photocopy was returned to me: ARCHIVO GENERAL DE INDIAS, 19 DIC. 2005, Entrada no. 2108. Frankly, I felt an odd achievement, an anointment of a kind, numeric only at the surface level, for my document, with my very signature, will forever be searchable by and linked to the library. A letter by me.

I am considering journey, travel, and work, occupation, both vocation and avocation. Almost every day in the late afternoon I have stopped at a small establishment, with the customary outdoor tables and chairs for *café con leche*, which in Spain is as good as it gets anywhere, where I am served by this giant, gap-toothed, redheaded waiter. Right or more likely wrong, as courteous and comfortable as he is, he does not seem to me like he should be wearing the white and black or an apron of the waiter. To my mind, it somehow does not match him. I imagine work in Sevilla *then*, employment, and I think, of course he would go to the New World.

And on my way to the Archivo I pass construction sites, even one going on next to the Archivo's Ministerio de Cultura building I enter each day, the men and I nodding in common *buenos* at each other, and I imagine seeing Francisco Pizarro's military leader Francisco de Carvajal, a huge and certainly cruel man who led his men into battles—always in full armor, never off his horse—"I am as big a target as any two of you, yet they do not hit me"—in Peru in his seventies, renowned for his tireless and sleepless energy, until he was executed and quartered in his eighties. I'm sure he was several of my own construction foremen and superintendents, and, I think, I imagine work *then*, and of course these men at this job would go.

But this is my morning. Oh sure, I do still have to wait. She just arrived when I first asked, and she couldn't see me right that minute. I'm over there, in the *sala*, I suggest. When I return, an hour later, we must have just missed each other, and she'll be back in a half hour or so. It is, I understand, unusual what I am asking. It is very uncommon. And she is very busy. So I have to be patient. The next time I hear her voice inside her office on the phone now, I'm that close. And, before I interrupt, she has to talk to this employee, and that one too. It is that tough *española* voice, aggressive, burned with and accelerated by nicotine. Until, finally, she has received me, and I am sitting in a chair in front of her. Not the *directora* herself, but the Jefe del Departamento de Referencias, the boss of the reference department. She has, it seems, my stamped and signed and numbered document on her desk in front of her. The *depósitos*, she says, have no old dust or dark corners, and it's not in a basement. She was quoting from my carefully written submission. She does not smile. I cannot, I recognize, bring up the little people scurrying, ask how many there are. It is, I try to say, a figure of speech. I have made a little list of questions, and I pull them out to leap over this pause, hoping that, maybe we can talk a little, converse, chat, relax. I want her to tell me a story, but her face seems, well, unenthusiastic, her voice defensive. Which isn't impolite. I don't take it that way, because that would be parallel to saying, for instance, a nun could be rude. So I think, well, maybe a couple easier questions about numbers of employees will lighten it up. No, not just reference librarians, I mean, all together. Around fifty. And the scanning machines—I make no mention of tortillas, nothing from me—and how many are on them, and how long does she expect such a project to take to scan it all? She shakes her head. She thinks I am criticizing their production? That I am writing a work review? I write, "a long, long time." In the pause I am deciding whether I should even bother to ask what the Archivo's most fascinating find is. And I wanted her to tell me what had been ripped off—they do have uniformed guards everywhere—what the most valuable loss has been. She's not going to see the human interest in either, so, instead, *bueno*, I'm ready, *vale*, let's go.

She moves fast. I am certain she was wondering, inside her mind, why it was I was walking with a gimpy foot, why it was hard for me to keep up. Though I meant to keep up, and I probably did so well she had no cause to notice. I did not want to slow her pace, I wanted to let her be herself. And I am sure, inside her mind, she was as curious about me as I might have been about her, you know, about where I was from, and where she was from, and so on. But we're both hurrying together, we're both excited for me to go *down there*. And when I tell her, out loud, so she'll hear me, "Those corners, that dust, it's all in my head, my imagination, a story I'm wanting, not The Truth," I'm not really sure she is sincerely listening to me. After we've gone under the mammoth chains, when we get to the front door of the public building, a coincidence—it's the actual *directora* herself coming into work!

She has on an ordinary brown wool coat, ordinary glasses, appears as much a mother and wife as most women who are the companions of those older men with the farsighted glasses and beret, in every respect a woman no one would ever suspect is the she who runs the Archivo de Indias. But she is short, half my size. Particularly small, even with a big winter coat on.

The *depósitos* are on the main floor, on the same tile and floor plan as what's seen publicly above, on the *planta primera*, where the tourists can see the displays. It occupies the same very high ceiling space of the Lonja building. The *legajos* themselves are stored in three rooms of metal bookcases which are collapsed, the aisles expandable by a hand turn of a wheel. There is the *directora's* office, there is a copy room, with copy machines, another where maps and plans and other large pieces are stored in long, flat metal cabinet drawers, and there is a restoration room, where the damaged papers go to be salvaged. There are a couple of men there, who are not tall, but not short. And another normal-size-range man who sits in a chair with a table, reading a daily newspaper, in the open space between the various rooms. He is responsible for finding the research requests from the *sala de investigadores*. But not many employees, it seemed to me. Are there others? It's coffee time, she tells me, and also a time of vacations. Yes, I nod, *por supuesto*. And thus, as fulfilled as I can be, I extend my *mil gracias* as she, staying behind, lets me through a twenty-foot barred gate near the front door entrance and exit.

Of course I'm suspicious of that convenient answer and that underworld gate. But then, I am a gimp. I am limited. *I am limited.* There is always less time, there is always more then. But with books, with my imagination, I travel out of my body's crumbling occupation of space and time, impossible distances, and I too discover many worlds *de maravilla* only few might believe or know but which are even true, even if it's in difficult English, Spanish, Latin, Greek, Alexandrian, Babylonian—more a "Babel" truth than what a fundamentalist with only two worlds believes or permits. There are limits, but there are the complexities that are not just two-dimensional or four-sided, or—in Sevilla, I read Borges—like hexagons, which there is learning, which is in libraries, is the Library. Borges writes:

Like all men of the Library, I have traveled in my youth; I have wandered in search of a book, perhaps the catalogue of catalogues; now that my eyes can hardly decipher what I write, I am preparing to die just a few leagues from the hexagon in which I was born. Once I am dead, there will be no lack of pious hands to throw me over the railing; my grave will be the fathomless air; my body will sink endlessly and decay and dissolve in the wind generated by the fall, which is infinite. I say that the Library is unending. The idealists argue that the hexagonal rooms are a necessary form of absolute space or, at least, of our intuition of space. They reason that a triangular or pentagonal room is inconceivable. (The mystics claim that their ecstasy reveals to them a circular chamber containing a great circular book, whose spine is continuous and which follows the complete circle of the walls; but their testimony is suspect; their words, obscure. This cyclical book is God.) Let it suffice now for me to repeat the classic dictum: *The Library is a sphere whose exact center is any one of its hexagons and whose circumference is inaccessible.*[*]

• • •

I went to the cathedral my last night, a Thursday, to visit the tomb of Colón. Instead there was a special mass with little girls dressed as angels, boys as shepherds, all bunched at the feet of a cardinal. The cathedral is, to say the least, cavernous, and for all the singing and ceremony and homily, it would be impossible for me, and not more than 200 others, to hear a word without the microphone. The difficulty I still had hearing was that I was distracted by the shine, tall and wide, of a spectacular altarpiece carved with more religious figures than I even knew existed, made so deafening by what I

---

[*]   Jorge Luis Borges, *The Library of Babel*, 1941.

could only assume was Aztec and Incan gold, melted trinkets and masks. But then a fog of incense alerted another sense, its jangle like an alarm clock, and the cardinal behind it, my eyes and ears shifted. The mass was a benediction of *imagenes navideñas*, and standing below me a little, little boy held up an object, a baby Jesus I think, no bigger than my thumb. When the father came, the red vestments, their nobility and formality and real sacred force, he sprinkled holy water on it, blessing it and the boy so personally, and he said he blessed us all, and I did feel so blessed, both sadness and joy.

And then my own last dinner. La Mezquita was my favorite restaurant in Santa Cruz, because who I took to be the manager always greeted me even when I was only passing by. I also liked eating there because he had a TV set on all the time, news or a program or *fútbol*. The day's special was my favorite, spinach with garbanzo beans. And I ordered *aceitunas*, the green Spanish olives that are as big as Mexican *limones*. What was on this night was the Spanish version of the quiz show *Who Wants to be a Millionaire?* The contestant wasn't, if you ask me, doing that well since he'd used up his lifelines before he got to what are supposed to be the harder questions, though two that he spent them on I wouldn't have gotten right if he hadn't. He was out of them when this one came: There were four names of Roman Emperors. Which country did they come from—Inglaterra, Italia, Grecia, or España? The owner was standing between me and another customer who was drinking a beer. The customer is saying, with certainty, it is not Italia, and it is not España. The owner isn't saying, and the game show host is pressing the contestant to make a decision. The customer with the beer makes his. Grecia, it has to be, he says. But me, I'd been to Mérida, and I can't help myself. España. It's that I had learned there were several Spanish emperors, and I knew for sure that Trajano, one of the names there, was one of them. The owner looks at me. España. He isn't sure, but he senses I must be right. When España blinks, not as the choice of the contestant either, the man with the beer both throws his arms up and slumps. I am from here! he cries. But not, I didn't say out loud, from Extremadura.

THE ONE WHO LEFT

This man—or woman in these migrant times—is also all of us who grew up without privilege or inheritance.

THE ONE WHO LEFT wasn't the only one sleeping on a stained twin mattress under a carpet remnant in the room near the stench of sewage, wasn't the only one making shadows as he passed by a single lightbulb dangling by a wire, who stepped over that worn-out dog, who liked to praise that dinner of beans and rice and chile, not the only one who shared a torn love seat to watch a fuzzy TV with so many brothers drinking beer and soda and sisters getting married, having babies, that crowd of aunts, uncles, cousins, nephews and nieces, not the only one with unfaded scars and some bad teeth, not one who complained about that so loud radio always somewhere, not the only one who could pick out the best used tires. He wasn't the only one loving a mother who wore that same housedress and apron, warming tortillas in the morning and early evening, that was still his beautiful mother. He was one who left and he will never stop loving her either. He had to leave behind a wife. The one who left had to leave behind his children. It was as though where he was going was a distant uncle's place, a man not blood, on his father's side, or it was the ex-husband of his godmother. Somebody close to somebody else, somebody known but who is not in the family. Connected to a man who has a successful construction business, or is a foreman, or is a landowner or knows a place to stay. A rich man or close or is just from "the states." He is the one many have seen drinking, laughing, talking loud in his language. He wouldn't agree to live in the nicest house in Mexico.

In "the states" there is work that pays and that is what the one who left needs and wants and he knows how to work, he is not afraid of any work, of earning. He has met good people, and bad people, and it is always dirty and mean, the same clothes no matter where or when or what. And that rich man does have lots of work. The one who left sweeps the sawdust and scrubs the cement and masonry tools and coils the hoses. He stoops low for the cinder blocks and he lifts a beam that has to be set high. He pushes the wheelbarrow and pounds spikes with a flattened waffle-face metal hammer and he pulls out pins with its claws. He hauls the trash scraps and he digs the plumbing trench. He always says yes and he means yes. He is a cheap wage, and he is quiet because he is far from home, as paperless as birth, and he not only acts grateful, he is grateful, because there is always worse at home.

The one who left is nobody special, and he knows it himself. There are so many others just like him, hungry, even hungrier once he's been paid. His only home is work, a job. His only trust, his only confidence, is the work, the job.

He lives near streets in "the states" that were the first ever in the city and are now the last repaired. He shops at markets where others who left go. He does not go to banks but of course he wants to. He does not have a driver's license but of course he wants one. He does not have a phone but of course he wants one. He wants his family to be with him.

He learned early to live like a cooling shadow at dusk and now he moves with almost a natural invisibility, carefully crossing into the light of night, not really seen when he's working in the sun.

He is someone who left his mother to get work. He left his wife to find work. He left his children to get work.

His citizenship is not in Mexico or in "the states" but is at a job.

He is not a part-time citizen, a temporary citizen.

He is a loyal citizen to a job, and he is a patriot of its country. He does not want to leave it in three years, or in six years. Like everyone else, he wants to become wealthy in his country.

BORDER PETROGLYPHS

Despite the topic of this piece, there was a lot of fun being with my compadre,
filmmaker Carlos Bolado, as we traveled both sides of border, from Tijuana to
Matamoros.

I'VE JUST BEEN ON a crew doing a documentary about the US-Mexico border. There were eleven of us: the director, an A and a B camera, a sound guy, an
actor, a writer, a still photographer, two producers (American and Mexican),
a set-design artist, and an assistant to the producer. We were two vans and a
red '65 Dodge Dart convertible, which is what I, the narrator, "drive" through
the film, from San Diego/Tijuana to Brownsville/Matamoros. We were all
from diverse ethnic backgrounds, though as passports go it was six Mexican,
five American. We were a group of well-established, credentialed members
of our respective cultural and artistic communities.

The intention of the movie was not investigative or politically topical,
not setting out to weed evil or quell injustice—not an exposé. Instead, it was
an almost personal exploration of the *frontera* and its *línea*, a journey to each
and every city and *pueblo* on either side. The camera and boom wanted to see
and hear what the border is, how it is, view it through images and impressions
of land and culture, voices and faces of people who are there, experiencing it.

Yet, of course, it was *la border*, *frontera*, of the United States and
Mexico. That is to say, we started to have hassles in the shoot that weren't
meant for our story.

Like when we wanted to talk to workers coming off a *turno*, a shift, from a *maquila* in Nogales, Sonora. Inside the sheet-metal hangar-like building, people were lined up silently waiting to get on a bus parked outside. The request was denied; no talking to the workers or filming inside, and the private security guard was quickly muttering into his walkie-talkie. A pickup with more uniforms arrived. Workers were warned not to speak to us.

I walked over to another building and spoke to a couple of workers from the distant states of Chiapas and Veracruz. I was interested in how their lives, now on the border, had changed, and they had nothing but contented things to say about their jobs and conditions and their move so far from home.

But, again, we were told to stop filming and to leave immediately. A hand slapped at the lens, and the cameraman, incensed, protested that he was on a public street and had every right, as a Mexican citizen, to film as he pleased. More security arrived; a pickup positioned itself to pen in our vehicles. We decided to leave, and after a brief cat and mouse on wheels for a few turns, we drove out. Except we were followed all the way, several miles, to the *aduana*, the border crossing, where the security people pulled up to men in green Mexican military uniforms armed with rifles. We crossed.

Don't you wonder what these other-side *mexicanos* were afraid of? Was it only the hackles and gaffs of unquestioned power?

That feathered display of power, cocky and mean as a drunk father, was not only on the Mexican side of the border. One morning we were one van and one camera, driving the state highway east of Judge Roy Bean's bar, named after the once-upon-a-time Only Law West of the Pecos. Our camera, hanging out the car window, filmed a border patrol SUV as it dragged a bundle of old tires along the soft dirt roads—their technique for tracking new people crossing illegally. Within a few minutes, we were pulled over. We explained how we were on our way to Seminole Canyon to film the Indian petroglyphs. The officer kept his distance from the driver's window, suspicious, and though he asked lots of questions, let us go. We didn't make the morning tour, so we planned to return later. When we were pulled over again on the ride back, it was two border patrol SUVs, and at least two more green-uniformed officers, their hands above their sidearms, standing backup as the officer we'd spoken to earlier examined our passports. He wrote down our names in a little notebook and went back to his truck's radio. For some time. He said he was passing along our names so that we could travel unhindered later.

Later that afternoon, on this same public highway, on our way to that guided petroglyph tour, we were pulled aside again, this time at the checkpoint. Told to get out, told to produce passports yet again, a gray-haired officer was loud in the director's face about what was it exactly he was doing here. That's when I said, "Excuse me, but I am an American citizen." The officer whipped his index finger within inches of my face, and with a blue, unblinking sneer, screamed at me how he'd talk to me when he decided to.

Which, of course, caused me to stop and think. There were five good-sized armed men surrounding the four unarmed us, their right hands cocked above their holsters, fingertips close enough for electrical static to jump from the handles of their weapons. The senior agent was—you could call it "impolitely"—discussing the border issues, as he saw it, with us. Where it is. How it is. Who he is, what he does. Where we were, who we were, who we were not. How if he thought we were doing any "counterintelligence," if he thought the story was the border patrol, he could "close us down," see what it was we got there on that video.

Though his roostering talk was addressed to the director, he looked at me often. That look of sizing up and threat. Come on, his aside glances said, I dare you to interrupt, to say anything.

And yes, he was right, I wanted to. Because he disgusted me. I hadn't wanted to go to blows with someone in years. I stared right back. You first, I decided. Almost smiling, my eyes never left his face, I stared back: You first.

These are the scenes that aren't going to be in the film. These are the clichéd news stories—the *migra*, Mexican police—that weren't meant for this documentary. It was what we wanted to skip. Yet, like *chinches* in the sheets of a dirty Nuevo Laredo motel bed, like mosquitoes swarming a humid swamp in Brownsville, they make bites that you hate for having to scratch, that won't go away quickly.

LAS MILPAS EN IOWA

Within FDR's Works Progress Administration (the WPA to all), there was an
additional program specifically for young American writers to go out across the
country and record the stories of the lives and work of our country's unseen people in
every state. A project that perfectly describes my own drive as a writer. It was called
the Federal Writers Project. Some of my favorite writers began there: Richard Wright,
Zora Neale Hurston, Nelson Algren, Studs Terkel, many more. In the mid-2000s a
revival of the idea came in the shape of an anthology called State by State. I was asked
by its editor to take where he was from, Iowa, not Texas or California, because he
couldn't do it. Which was perfect for me because I had already dreamed of doing a long
piece on corn.

WHAT DO I VISUALIZE when I think of Iowa except, like everyone, a
cartoon image of it: corn and pigs and big healthy farmers who eat hearty
American food. I'm on my flight out of the Dallas–Fort Worth hub, on a
regional ER4 jet, a fifty-seater, and I've got the single side on aisle 12, the
emergency exit, with the extra legroom. The two-seat side on my right is
empty up to the very last minute, when a huge, healthy man moves into
it before takeoff. He has to be six-five easy, 250 minimum, but I wouldn't
call him fat, any more than I'd dare to call the Red Sox's David Ortiz fat.
Medically too heavy, he's not any way weak or soft. He's a friendly guy too,
smiles at me like we're onto it like a stash, us big guys, and all those others
are not—might as well enjoy the ride, he tells me. He reads a newspaper

slowly, the not-very-taxing *USA Today*, though there's a lot in it, lots of sections, and at least he's reading, that skill becoming more and more rarefied. What I see are his hands. Oversized too, wrinkled and thickened by work. Up above a few rows is another Iowan. A man so huge I can't see how he isn't making the plane dip. There are so many other passengers who are not small on this small plane. Iowa, or I'm used to flights out of shorter cultures?

When we land, I call my friend Mando, who is due to pick me up. "*El águila ha tortillado.*"

I joke. Lately we've been stuffing bad words into a tortilla. "I'll be there in ten, *tortillero.*" As I stand and move to the aisle, not having to watch my head as much as my row 12 partner, out of nowhere an older woman appears two rows ahead on the two-seat side. She is staring at me like she overheard. I didn't see her before because, seated, her head was beneath the headrest, hidden. *Con una cara morena*, a dark face classic of historic Mexico, she would make a perfect tourist painting. Even standing, she wasn't much higher than the headrest. We file out, through the exit billows, into the airport market corridor, signs with arrows from the ceilings. She is ahead of me, walking slow, many looping around her. She is looking side to side, and I when I reach her side it seems to me she is waiting for me to catch up. "*¿Vas a las mochilas?*" she asks me. I assume she means the baggage area, so I tell her that and to just follow me. "*¿A la mochila?*" She's almost frightened about getting lost, because a couple of times we've had to curve around people and make a turn. Yes, straight ahead, it's a walk, it's usually a long walk in airports, it's more in front of us, and we're going there, I have baggage too, I have a suitcase. This appeases her; she's walking faster, I'm walking slower, we travel side by side. It's nothing but summer from below Dallas and above Iowa and to the east and west, it's too warm even inside, and she is wearing a thin pink sweater over her flowery black dress that seems to bury her shoes. Her *trenza*, her black and gray braid, reaches below the middle of her back.

She's from Guadalajara, and it's her first time here, not Iowa, first time in the United States, and it was only five hours. She's still tense. Thinking maybe it was immigration or customs lines she's worrying about, I tell her that she passed through that once, when she went through Dallas—thinking maybe this is a worry. And she's never been on an escalator. I have to show her. I want to hold her hand, but don't want to be too forward. I have to tell her when to step when we get to bottom. Her hop is like a five-year-old's, though less excited. And when we make the final turn, the aluminum baggage claim area visible, I practically can't keep up with her. And as we reach it, right then walking through the glass doors is her family, probably her son's, her daughter-in-law, a granddaughter the oldest and most shy to see her, a grandson maybe ten, and a newborn. They all hug and then she is holding the baby grandchild, and she and the women step off to the side, while the father and son, in sports shorts and American football jerseys and sneakers, both with buzzcuts a month's worth long, wait near me as the suitcases circle.

●●●

This is about the tortilla. This is about corn grown in Iowa. This is about the people who are in the *campos* of Iowa picking the vegetables and walking the cornfields. Those people are Mexican people. They are of the culture where hand-ground masa was first patted into tortillas and, because of that, it is said that the physical body of any mexicano is at least half corn. They are from the civilization that worshipped the corn plant as a god—in some regions, such as what became known as Guatemala, the God, the image of God—and they are from the soil and nation where this corn we all have learned to eat and to feed as grain for healthy livestock was first developed and harvested 5,000 years ago. They are the people who now are driven here, because even corn, and the tortilla, is going up in price since the 1990s NAFTA treaty, and subsidized corn in the United States is cheaper to import, and the demand increases its value to the corporate farmers in Mexico. Because corn has become an ethanol fuel industry, its hybrid grain is even more wanted. In Mexico, the ordinary *milpas*—cornfields—are shrinking in size, and those people who traditionally worked them can't make enough to survive in their villages and so they are leaving, like animals in a drought, going to the big cities to find jobs, and they are crossing the border because that is where most jobs are. They have come even to Iowa because they will be hired and work in meat-packing plants cheaply, hard, and they work in the fields cheaply and hard. And as they work *las milpas* in Iowa to do as their culture has done for thousands of years, anti-immigration ideologues bash them for spoiling what they see as a field of dreams as clean and pure as Iowa butter, as nostalgic as baseball, as all-American as Kevin Costner.

How to make the commercial tortilla: There are fifteen fifty-five-gallon drums, and every night the corn soaks four to five hours, bubbling under fifteen burners, and they are stirred with paddles like those you would use to propel a rowboat. After a while, using a can of a measured size, lime is scooped out of sacks and mixed in and stirred and stirred. A foam like from the ocean rises, which means it is working, breaking down the corn right, so it is healthy to eat. Then the corn rests a few hours. Warm still, tin buckets with holes in the bottom both take out the corn and drain the water so it can be ground in the *molino*, where stones turn it into masa. Now a ball the size of a watermelon, it is fed between twin rollers which flatten the dough onto a conveyor, where it is cut. This raw tortilla falls onto a traveling grill, cooking one side, then falls to another, flipping it to its other side for grilling, until it drops onto one more belt which drops it onto a cooked stack. Women pick them up from there, counting them onto a waxed paper. They wrap the paper up around this counted pile and flip the package over—in, say, Corpus Christi, Texas, it might be Charro Tortillas printed on the paper—and stack them in a box for delivery.

In Iowa, in mid-July, the leaves of the corn stalks are waxy, veined, like a narrow palm, and the two sides of each leaf peel and fall away from its spine as they grow out—water can funnel right into that crease like halved paper, run down the stalk, drench the shallow roots—until they are long enough to droop delicately, tenderly, at their end points. Their stalks are bamboo thin and knuckled and, here, already at least as tall as I am, and I can see through them and past. A green patina rustles more than in the leaves. It is a light casting through, like a mist. And it's the blue sky you begin to see better. Blue as an imagined heaven, blue that isn't only sky but is this earth, as close as the tallest green stalks and leaves touching it, and it is, noticeably, more blue because it rests on top of the cornfield.

•••

Blocks to the east of the golden domes of the Iowa state capitol building is the most Mexican neighborhood in the city. Not many years ago this wasn't so. Now when you drive E. 14th, you see a street whose appeal is to people who need transportation to and from jobs, the used car and truck dealers, auto repair shops, parts houses, tire stores, and corner stores with the cheapest gas prices, and, alongside hamburger joints and diners, taquerías. Here in this Iowa now, the Mexican businesses bear names that are tourist-recognizable and famed—Aztec, Los Pinos, Fiesta Cancún, El Tequilero. The newest market, La Tapatía, is doing so well that the area around it has expanded into a mall. And it is busy inside, lots of employees and checkout stands, these shoppers wanting Mexican products—beans, rice, fideos, cheeses, chiles dry in bulk and packaged, spices, sauces and moles, cooking oils, crackers and cookies, meat and poultry cut their style, still hot carnitas and chicharrón, fruits and vegetables we Americans know well and also those like yucca and prickly pear and guayaba, and coconut, and sliced white bread, and piles and stacks of tortillas. I want corn tortillas and buy a couple of packages listing the preservative-free three ingredients only—lime, corn, water—and a paleta of watermelon *con chile*.

On the way out, in that small entry and exit room that all markets have now for throwaway papers and bulletin boards and charcoal and hand-shopping baskets, there are two stacks of individually scissored slips from an Eagle Eye Detasseling, one hot orange, another a fluorescent green, looking for workers to "walk the cornfields" and take off the *espigas*, the tassels. It goes on, *El trabajo empezara por el 10 de julio. Venga a la orientación el lunes 2 de Julio a las 6 de la tarde atrás de la tienda la favorita*, says the green one, while the orange one, also with a date, adds the word *seguro*, "safe," to its *HAY TRABAJO* heading, making clear that this is a contractor who will hire people who have immigration documents or don't. Though that July date has already passed, I go to La Tienda Favorita, a small, unintimidating Mexican meat market in the heart of this downtown community, to see if anyone there might know something. The owner and his son say maybe they were there one morning, but they don't remember exactly, clearly not something sticking in their minds as important or noticeable. On a counter near the local Latino newspaper, another clipped slip, that same green, with another line of information in bold type: *necesito 30 trabajadores para la espiga.*

I walk over to the capitol. Capitols are the cathedrals of government, teaching us hallowed doctrine and belief and history. Iowa's United States story began in 1803 when President Thomas Jefferson bought it from the French—in the Louisiana Purchase—and began distinguishing a state history in 1846. It's on a stairway wall between the first and second floors of the capitol building where Iowa represents its philosophical genesis in a five-panel mural by artist Edwin Blashfield called *Westward*: A family of pioneers is traveling west in a covered wagon, a prairie schooner. Angels floating behind them carry a steam engine and an electric dynamo, while the angels in front have baskets of seeds to drop. The angel at the farthest front holds up a large book open at the middle, pointing it like it's a headlight to see in the dark, yet at the same time it seems meant to be seen by anyone ahead of them, as though it were a sacred and irrefutable commandment, both proof and inspiration.

A few miles away, at the Iowa Corn Promotion Board offices, a generous information coordinator gives me a lesson on the differences between field corn and edible corn (how each silk thread we see when we husk is like an umbilical cord to each individual kernel on the cob), and the names of each (sweet, pop, flint, dent, flour, broom, waxy maize, pod). Also there is the latest biogenetic corn, or what some want to call "frankencorn"— she chuckles at that, dismissing the criticism. It's only good, only the latest change in corn that has always been cross-fertilized. Just as some are developed to be more drought resistant, others to bear more kernels or to mature in shorter growing seasons for different altitudes, these are genetically altered to be immune to, for instance, certain pesticides or soil fungi. Corn, which evolved from the wild *teocinte* of Central Mexico, she explains, has always been cross-fertilized by hand (and monarch butterflies) and has evolved for the times and the region. What does she say about the history of *maiz* being sacred, a god in early Mexico? She has no idea why it was worshipped.

On University Avenue, some blocks from Drake University, it's dinnertime at a lunch truck. Silver like an Airstream and hooked up like one too, it is moored on this empty lot, aluminum poles and thin rope and white plastic roof making a cabana-like porch at the order window, wooden picnic benches under it. The food is Mexican, not overstuffed TexMex, so the *tacos al pastor* are on traditionally small corn tortillas, delicate, with a slice of avocado and with a wedge or two of *limón*. I get a bottle of pineapple Jarritos soda and sit at a table next to where a man wearing an LA Dodgers baseball cap sits too. I open the conversation by asking about the white paint splattered all over his clothes, if he's a painter. He does everything, he says. He works on a rancho not too far from here. He says it's the rancho belonging to the man who runs el Mercy, the hospital. He does everything on it, not just paint: He works the yard, the pool, takes care of the horses, which they don't ride. He's all by himself out there, he says. An estate, I think, not a ranch. He's from Michoacán, from the city of Morelia, and he'll complete three years in August. Two more years, he tells me, and he'll go home. Doesn't everyone say that? Yes, but he means it. He's lonely. He wants to go home. Why does he do it? To better his family. They are there, waiting for him. I pause, finally ask if he knows any farmer, anyone hiring workers for *las milpas*. Oh yes, he is sure these jobs are around. He suggests a market around the corner. He says there will be ads in the Spanish newspapers they sell there. My eyes go down the street his words direct me to. I have to remind myself that this is Iowa.

• • •

My own manifest destiny comes as a message left on my answering machine back in Texas, and it's through Proteus, a migrant farmworkers outreach program, that I will find a farmer's cornfields. Reluctant to dial anybody's number at six in the morning, I do anyway. On that other side of the line, it sounds more like wide-awake noon, voices and voices beyond the one confirming, saying come on. My directions are 80 east, 218 south, 22 east, 70 south, and I can't miss it.

Interstate 80: So many cars are new or almost, washed, and the trucks—eighteen-wheelers, not only FedEx, UPS, Walmart—they too are washed clean traveling an uncluttered, unlittered highway that feels so much more lane-roomy than it really is. Iowa in this July is more a hobbit-land of unwild, luxuriant green. It seems all the land is planted—soybean is the other big crop—but it is the cornfields that dominate, fields both flat and contoured up hills in curved and squared lines, a vast, groomed Versailles gardens.

On the two-lane 22, a sheriff pulls me over for driving 30 mph through an intersection. Yes, sir, I saw the eighteen-wheeler in my rearview mirror, and that's why I didn't slow down more, because I'm afraid I'm going to miss my turn. . . . When it seemed like too far a few miles further, I pull over beside a man and woman, Iowans from head to toe except they're speaking Spanish, and she directs me across the road, right where the sign, Bell's Melons, I should've seen myself is maybe half a block back up.

I go through the warehouse to get to the office, passing twelve-foot stacks of empty pallets, on the vast, mostly empty cement floor, only one loaded with boxes of vegetables. It's being plastic-wrapped off a spool by a couple of men in overalls who don't speak Spanish, watched by a couple of men who only do. Inside the small office, women are handling clipboards and pencils and answering phones ringing from every corner. Terri Bell, with her reading glasses in heavy use and a handful of colored markers, exasperated yet still kind to me, is organizing time sheets and grocery store lists of what's still needed for the campesinos' lunches. Her husband, Tom, he's the one who comes for me. Wiry and quick, his only move is for-ward, and he tells me right away I'll have to follow him around. It's the first day the men—H2A workers, meaning they have papers and are hired temporarily—arrived on buses from Monterrey, Mexico, last night, and this is their first full day here. Already running, and even as he's on the phone, he hands me the same cream *gorra* he gives these men—a hat with SYNGENTA across it, the international seed corporation—and a red bandanna with his own business name and logo—Bell's Detasseling, a basket with three ears of shucked ripe corn standing tall. On the way and into his red Chevy 4x4, he tells me he pays $500 for their round trip, and he's hired around 450 from early July to early August. He pays $9.95 an hour, charges $11.20 a day for food. They work the cornfields, and also pick beans, cucumbers, watermelon—to name a few. Why not illegals? It's not worth the risk. Why not Americans? He can't find them.

We drive on a paved road parallel to the highway, a neighborhood of what once upon a time were one- or two-bedroom workers' homes, now squeezed in by two or three trailer homes mounted on cement foundations. We stop at what is like a compound, outside the kitchen/mess hall add-on to a brick schoolhouse—a banner is over the stoves and grills, SUPER COCINA LOS AMIGOS—where employees are packing ice chests of lunches and counting how many meals go in each, getting the numbers right. As Tom squints over a problem with the ice machine's outdoor runoff hose, I go over to a picnic bench where a group of men, young and older, are sitting. Beyond them, on an open field, a few men kicking around a soccer ball. They all go eyes up and quiet at me once I'm close, like I bear the latest news. Instead, I find out that they are all from Durango. Have they done this work before? Half of them say no. The one who seems the eldest, a straw hat, dark skin weathered, he says he's done it most of his life. How did he find out about this, in Iowa? Just heard. But how, exactly? They look around at one other, nobody sure what to say. Do you hear about it . . . like, maybe you would gossip? They laugh at that. One heard it from this one next to him, he's the one who told that one, thus. Isn't Durango a long trip from Monterrey? They all shrug, the questions making them, too, more conscious. You just took a bus there? They say yes and nod, are now smiling at me. They took a bus to Monterrey, they signed some papers, and a bus brought them here.

The school building is where Tom Bell went to elementary school. Now it's been converted into a bunkhouse for his workers—all men, only men. At the top of the first stairs in, there are old couches and a TV set up in the corner—a *novela* is playing—and then we pass through a small room, maybe fifteen to twenty bunk beds, all just built of fresh-cut 2 × 4 and 2 × 6 boards. Like a dad pleased by his son's expensive college graduation, Tom shows me how much he's transformed the school: Where we stand used to be above the gym floor, where you could watch a game, and down below was where the courts were. Down below now are maybe a hundred more bunk beds, all occupied. Clothes are already hanging off them, a few have already washed underwear and socks and laid them out to dry on the head- and footboards. In a far corner, another "lounge" area of old couches, a TV up high, with cable, that same *novela*. The showers are gym-like, the sink for hands and face and teeth, and probably for rinsing underwear is a room-length trough with a dozen or so faucets. The walls and ceilings show the new remodel, all the new studs exposed, sheathed by pressed-wood, low-grade ply. Windows are open. A monster fan is mounted up high to blow in more air. Iowa? Right now it looks and sounds and—the kitchen is right next to this big space—smells like it's Mexico.

Tom doesn't even know a word of Spanish. What does he think about all these people here?

He loves these people, he says, and he's proud to do them right. He owns a condo in Manzanillo. When all this gets done, in the winter, he and his wife relax there for a month. He loves it.

Becky's my ride to a cornfield being walked—it's known by a field number, the digits as natural and recognizable to them as a pet's name. Her blue pickup loaded with iced sodas and a chest of *lonches*, she wants to know why it has to be her who takes me and she isn't entirely joking. She's a big Iowa woman, a '60s-era grown up, born and raised not far away, rooted to the driver's seat. Her tattoos barely seen under the browned sunburn of her fleshy upper arms, she also works biker gatherings and just retired from the clerical staff at the university. It's a few ranch roads to where we go, a route that crosses the rich Iowa River and would lead to Muscatine. Talking about the men bunking in the school, she says she cannot imagine the raunch of it—sweat and dirty socks, snores, farts from those beans. Who'd be able to stand all these men? she asks. Then again, she might, she tells me after a pause, smiling dirty-minded.

We pull onto a dirt farm road where dust rises from behind and stop alongside the cornfield, near the rented yellow school bus that transports the workers. Tom's son is there to wave at us from his pickup—he's on the phone, as busy as his dad. Men too short to be seen inside the tall corn jungle begin to emerge. No factory whistle, and it's not like a construction site either, where at a certain hour everyone stops everything. Mostly in pairs, the campesinos exit slowly, unrushed, from the world of *zurcos*, rows, bandannas under their hats to wrap their necks, bandannas and dark glasses masking their faces—a few have mosquito netting—and long-sleeved shirts and gloves, their *mochila*—a day bag or a plastic store bag to carry an extra shirt or rain poncho or some rubber boots and their own personal valuables—slung on their back or in hand. On their belts hangs a rubber clip for a soda bottle to hang and carry water. The gloves and bottle hook are gifts from Bell's Detasseling. They get their *lonches* from the ice chests—a caldo of pork, pineapple, and bell pepper, a fresh jalapeño, tortillas still warm in foil. A few men go inside to sit on the soft seats there. A few sit against a side of the bus, in a slant of shade. I go over to three who rest at the back, to the Igloo cooler, taking their time before they eat.

I tell them how they all look like Subcomandante Marcos coming out from the jungle.

After a moment to absorb my joke, they look at each other until they finally grin. They are from Monterrey, young, though one must be closer to thirty than the other two. None of them have crossed the US-Mexican border before now. Only one of them has worked in agriculture previously, but this isn't hard work except for the hours—though it isn't so hot yet, even with the long-sleeved shirts that they have to wear, the fields aren't too muddy, the mosquitoes haven't gotten so bad yet. Jobs are hard to find over there and it's never enough. The youngest one talks about working in garages and restaurants. There is a lot of danger to do other things. The older one says how running *movidas* might seem good for a little bit, but it's not worth the trouble. This work is good for them, even if it's only a month. We are looking at the sky, more Hollywood design and concept than Iowa, the clouds too white, too flawlessly shaded gray to be believed, too beautiful. The older one asks about me and I tell them how I was born in Los Angeles and worked construction. Even through their mirror glasses, I see their eyes go starry. I mention El Paso and the capital, Austin, and how in Dallas, and how in Houston, and it's as though I am speaking of mythical lands. I gesture to the east and tell them over there is where Chicago is, very close. The youngest one jokes how fast they could get there. The other two aren't even considering it, though the third, the quiet one, takes a couple of steps in that direction to see that much closer. This is good for now, the older says. It's what they have. After a pause, the younger one returns, sincerely, *así es la vida*.

We drive to another field, more masked campesinos breaking through the corn jungle rows unexcitedly, unhurried, to take lunch. The conversations are muted. Music they like and don't, other places they've been. Muted, like they are faraway. On this field the crew chief has them leave their *mochila* at the beginning of each row, and all but three have been picked up. When most have finished eating, two of the stragglers appear and nod, pleased, about where to find the lunches. Twenty minutes later, the last one, Oscar, unmasked, finally comes out just as these other two go back to work. Maybe he's eighteen, maybe twenty-one. Unlike all the others I've seen so far he is overweight in that soft manner of a good boy from El Paso or San Antonio, playing too many video games in front of a TV, with sodas, candies, and Doritos. He's slow because he is tired but also much more—lost, miserable, mom-sick—and he can barely speak, though he does, a thank you when he is told where he will find his *lonche*. When he is done eating—maybe he does take an entire half hour, but certainly no more than—he ends his lunch break in the same self-absorbed, unselfconscious way he began, stepping back, like his feet hurt, to a line of *zurcos* where the others have been out of sight for some time already.

The rows of these *milpas* have been mowed earlier so that they are all an even height. They are arranged so that one male plant from one seed will pollinate at least the two females, grown from a different seed, on either side of it, so that the layout is four rows of females, a male row, four female, a male, and so on. The leaves of the first male stalk are sprayed a Day-Glo orange—the men must know which it is because its *espigas*, its tassels, are the only ones that must be left untouched: It is their pollen that will reach the female silks below which will grow the kernels on the cob, a new, third seed which will be harvested. Though corn carries with it both male and female parts, what the campesinos are doing is castrating the ones in the rows of four, yanking off their male parts. On a first pass, men pull this shaft out of its stalk, the one blooming an unpollinating tassel, from its node, effectively castrating the plant, leaving the *cañajote* beneath. The tassel pops out easily, a juiced, fleshy pop that sounds not unlike cracking a knuckle, and is dropped onto the dirt of the *zurco*. After a second pass through, there is yet another pass, this one crosswise, made by a more seasoned *chequeador*, a checker, who looks for misses. Wrapped in the same leaf husk as the ripe female corn on the cob we know, peeled away it looks much like young rye or wheat, only deep green, and huskier. When left to bloom, with the sun on it, the green becomes more golden, the yellowish pollen sticky, though not as sticky as the white female silks waiting beneath. The field has to be 99.7 to 99.8 percent detasseled for the crop to germinate the exact corn seed that is hoped for.

Five thousand years of walking *las milpas* in Mexico, the descendants of those people are now in Iowa, most American of American states, and walking cornfields, attending to this cross-fertilization work considered spiritual way, way back then. Iowa's Mexicans are only a little more aware of corn's history than those in Iowa are. It's as though the migration of the Mexican deity itself has finally summoned its native worshippers to tend to it, populating the soil it grows in. I ask Becky: Ten, fifteen years ago it would be high school and college boys and girls from towns here. It was not only a summer ritual, but a good income for the summer. Now you have to hire as many as you can because only half stay with it. They are too hot. They are too sunburned. One doesn't want to work past 2:00 p.m., another says she can't. One wants to rest a day because he got too tired the day before. It's the weekend. Or it's because it was just the weekend and he wants to sleep in. One has to babysit on certain days, and then maybe the next she just doesn't feel like showing up at all. And then there's the other, smaller issues. If someone's litter from lunch gets left behind, for instance, you ask one to pick it up. It's not mine is the answer. Pick it up anyway. It's not mine. Okay, but pick it up anyway. I didn't leave that. Just pick it up! There is no litter in these *campos*, and these *mexicanos* are always polite and they work until they are told it is time to stop. There are a lot more cornfields than there used to be, and there wouldn't be enough Iowa people around who could work the fields even if.

· · ·

To be at the school buses at 4:30 a.m. you have to get up and go to them earlier. It's dark then, the rising sun in the east an ember of blue light so pure it calms all in its sight, the only nature visible except when a stray head- and taillight flash by on its sizzling highway. The buses idling, the campesinos, their *mochilas* hung on shoulders, hats on, their work IDs looped to their neck, find their way inside the one they are assigned. So effortless and still, it's almost like nature itself. A couple of men greet me when those men have gone, walking out of the kitchen with a styrofoam coffee cup steaming. The first one is named Raúl and he's originally from Big Spring, Texas. Been in Conesville for so many years now he's for Iowa football and thinks this year they'll beat Texas. His job is as a translator, and he tells me it's the best job he's ever had. When his wife and two teenage children drive up in a pickup—they're working for the Bells too—he introduces them all to me, switching into English. His wife, a native Iowan, he met when he first came up here for work. His children, sleepy as they are, are nothing but polite. They are Iowans.

When they take off, Alejandro steps beside me. Alejandro is the man Tom Bell probably counts on the most. Alex is what they call him. This is his fifth year here now and he is employed at least a month before the other workers and at least a month after, always the longest. When three men pile out of the bunkhouse at 5:00 a.m. it's Alex who is shaking his head at them—he told everyone 4:30, and now there's no ride until 6:30. They wait over on the school steps.

Alejandro is from Nayarit, which is on the Pacific Ocean side of Mexico, a long way from a bus depot in Monterrey. He's picked everything, he tells me proud, every fruit and every vegetable. Just before he came here, he'd been working in a sugarcane factory back home. This is a good job, he says. He'll come back as often as he can. Mr. Bell treats him well, treats them all well. When someone can't take it, can't make it out there? It happens, and they find something around the grounds for them to do. It all works out.

It is dawn now, blue gray, more people, more talk, no more indoor lights needed. Alejandro yells over to those guys sitting. He tells them they can get a ride in a pickup that just pulled up, that it's going to their field, and reminds them not to forget to check in with their crew chief. Six-feet five-inches high, Alejandro is as tall and lean as the healthiest Iowa cornstalk, as native to México as *maiz*, and he is right in the middle of the field of dreams.

THE FIRST RESIDENT OF
BELKEN COUNTY

The purpose of the '60s Chicano Movement was to make the clear point that we are not the immigrants to this region and country's land, but those who came from Kentucky, Tennessee, and Kansas to Texas and the American West are.

I GREW UP IN the capital of the celebrity world, Los Angeles, where the sun rose to shine on us, not only me even if it seemed so when I looked up, where ocean waves, not that far away when I ditched school and hitch-hiked, lapped the shores like sweet, romantic kisses, where the blackened nights were white-lined boulevards full of starry head- and taillights cruising low and slow, checking for the good and the bad, left and right more important than up ahead. I grew up where "cool" began, where music that mattered came to make it, the dip and sway stopping only when I was asleep, and where movies and their really important screens were actually big and curtained. All this was *mine*. This glam and glory spilled onto me and the hood I came up in, where I met the best-looking girls, I was in the baddest rides, and I was up against the ugliest, most dangerous dudes who I could take if . . . if it weren't for the fact that *that* LA was, maybe, as lasting as a movie star sighting (which was—are you kidding?—never where I came up), a dreamland that had little to do with my life.

There are lots of LAs, and mine was really a neighborhood that was cut through for the newest freeway, meaning not just cheap, dispensable land and people, but story. The heroic fable that ran in my head was one that warped significantly from larger facts, and only incidentally overlapped with the name of the city. When the truth penetrated, it was worse than being the earth and finding out the sun wasn't swooning around it. I was, at most, a fleck of dust on this planet that was but a fleck of dust in the huge sky. I realized that, as LA goes, story accuracy aside, mine wasn't of much unique interest either. We've all heard that perennial *who am I?* I began with *where*, which came with a *how*, as in, what kind of mess did I get myself into? My East LA dad lived more like a cliché Mexican, or German, forty-nine years at one job—beginning at age thirteen, interrupted only once by the Marine Corps—until he got laid off in his sixties. My mom, who I grew up with, was born in Mexico but was nobody's stereotype but for the drinking one. Single, she wanted to dress for a Parisian nightlife.

Brush aside lots of landlocked, unimpressive jobs that came and went lots more often than my drives between LA and El Paso, toss broken lineage issues that were my familial inheritance, and fast forward to the mind's homing instinct: Just say I began by researching this large *where* through its big stories. I climbed the stacks for the too far away, the Naipaul from Trinidad, the Achebe from Africa, of course the Russian, German, and French (Dostoyevsky, Hesse, Camus) (no British for me—that language barrier too great), and then I went south to Fuentes in Mexico City, Vargas Llosa in Lima, García Márquez in Macondo. I wanted to be Beckett, old, wise, funny. I lived with Chuang-tzu in China. Rulfo's scorched earth altered my reading DNA, made me there and farther away at the same time. I finally started looking around nearer. I read Wright's leftie Chicago, Kerouac's New York to San Francisco and back, and Kesey's fierce rivers, giant trees Oregon. I read LA: Bukowski—I wasn't a drunk and didn't want to get that ugly. Fante—sorry dude, you're good, but I have problems with your Mexican gal bs. Didion—I was certain she would not approve of my kind dating her daughter. In El Paso I got closer still—Mariano Azuela, John Rechy, Ricardo Sánchez—but I wasn't a Mexican national, I wasn't gay, I'd never been a pachuco or in the joint.

I was living in an El Paso YMCA, financially zeroed, in 1977. That's where I was exactly. Whatever the cause, I was the closest to "home" I'd gotten. It was like I was smelling the first musky wisp of desert rain, and I needed the rain. My girlfriend (who would become my wife) had given up on me and moved back to Eagle Pass. She took a job at Crystal City High School. Cristal, in the Spanish pronunciation as it's known by *raza*, was the source and beginning of the Chicano movement in Texas, beginning in the late '60s. And there my girlfriend had found a book in its library, and she . . . though I still have it today, let's say she checked it out for me. It was *Estampas del valle y otras obras*, and it was by the author Rolando R. Hinojosa-S*, a name so convoluted it seemed more from a Borges short story. A bilingual text, on the surface it was as it stated it was, "sketches" or vignettes of the valley, which is to say the Río Grande Valley, far closer than Argentina. It was in this book, by this writer, Rolando Hinojosa, that I found my lost *where*.

· · ·

How can a person—a man whose internal demand was to become a writer—born a few handfuls of urban miles from the Pacific Ocean, find "home" in a rural community one or two handfuls of ranch miles from the river that was the Texas border between the United States and Mexico? In college, back in the day, I was lucky enough to go to events that brought César Chávez to speak. I loved going, but I felt as connected to the farmworkers movement as a high-rise ironworker with a spud wrench in a field

---

* His full name is Rolando Hinojosa-Smith. His last name goes with the usage common in the Spanish and Latin American tradition, with father's last name first and then the mother's maiden name. The hyphen is a North Americanism. It is ordinary, especially in Latin America, to simplify names to first name and father's last. Thus, Rolando Hinojosa is what is used on all of his books post-Estampas and is how he is referred to by virtually all who write about his work or know him personally.

of artichokes. I really had no idea how broccoli or carrots grew or where they came from but a supermarket—and who ate vegetables not already in cans? I was also around to see performances (later, not original) of the agitprop plays, the "actos," written by Luis Valdez and his Teatro Campesino. As traveling tent theater, they were great and huge fun. Though the characters, all recognizable, were purposely exaggerated figures I knew well—suckered *mexicanos*, sleazy used car salesman and bosses, sellouts and thieves—they were not city enough for me. What I did recognize were Chicanas and Chicanos who could act and support a poor worker's cause.

•••

In Américo Paredes's exquisite classic, *With His Pistol in His Hand*, a defense of Texas Mexican history, the Anglo heroes of Texas, their Rangers, weren't so John Wayne tall or noble when it came to the treatment of *raza*, and, by the way, besides the injustice based on their ignorant misunderstanding of horse terminology, *tejano* Gregorio Cortez, the wrongly accused hero, could ride the hell out of them, allowing time to prove his innocence—and eat up enough time on the run to inspire a ballad documenting his story and the culture's pride.

Though both writers produced works that were paeans to Mexican Americans and their culture, both writers (not to imply there weren't others) models for activist writing, the focus of each was what the people were up against to survive. Yet it wasn't until Hinojosa's *Estampas*—his characters living in the Río Grande Valley of Texas—what in his later books he would name more specifically Klail City, within the county called Belken—that another, seemingly simple assumption became the setup for his fictional land and its residents:

> In the Valley, in this Valley covered by ranches and towns,
> there are families in hiding. But make no mistake, they're not
> doing it out of shame. They're hiding out because they know
> who they are. (Cipriano Villegas Malacara, 1855–1933)

Senator, when one of those Valley Mexicans says *yesterday*, he probably doesn't mean "yesterday" as such. Like as not, he's most likely talking about 1850 or 1750, even. It's hard to say; I can't understand 'em myself, half the time. (Capt. Rufus T. Klail, 1850–1912)

Permit me to adjust and expand on what the deceased character (from Hinojosa's later novel, *Claros varones de Belken*), Mr. Villegas Malacara, had to say—those unashamed families, though hidden from view from the outside looking in, are clearly not in hiding. From the ground, from inside, they are far from unseen by anyone who's there. *This* is what the entirety of Hinojosa's writing, from *Estampas* onward, assumes and what then proceeds to make clear to the smallest conversational detail. That the culture and community exists and knows it has from at least 1750 was not what was new here either. What was, startlingly, was that Hinojosa, paying no attention to the dominant culture beyond, taking that for granted in the same manner of the residents of his fictional city, says this: It is there now too, still, it didn't and doesn't stop existing when readers look away, or when a searchlight dims on those issues or struggles, large and small, national and regional, criminal or political. Belken County is as autonomous and singular as Texas itself, no more or less dependent than any other small country, most unavoidably the "counties" in the north. Not to say that Klail doesn't go unaffected; just that its history, its story, is not only what exists in connection to whatever the current moment is with the powerful Anglo culture in the nation both call home.

What I saw in Hinojosa's *Estampas* wasn't my own family tree, except for what was just like it. What I saw in his land wasn't like mine whatsoever, except it was the closest I'd encountered to what was. And I'd never seen it anywhere else before. His neighborhood, rural Belken County, wasn't much like the city streets I grew up on, but, especially as a writer, it was the first time I'd ever seen people where I was then (and now) and where I'd come from, the same as where he was. Yes, I'm saying Los Angeles and El

Paso—and Corpus Christi, San Antonio, McAllen, Brownsville, Laredo, Eagle Pass, Del Rio, Albuquerque, Las Cruces, Denver, Tucson, Phoenix, Santa Ana, Riverside—were in the same country where his residents lived and had lived. And here is what, for me, was most important: His characters confirmed an existence of these people as I found them—hidden in plain sight, unknown everywhere around, yet seen everywhere anyone in the American Southwest looked.

In LA, as in El Paso, as in Klail, the most common people have long family histories in the United States. They are working people, though the jobs are ordinary ones we know every day and, like the people themselves, are taken for granted and ignored. They work in stores as salespeople and offices as clerks and secretaries, in pharmacies and grocery stores, outdoors on soil or on rangeland. They are butchers and seamstresses, business owners and government employees, or at buildings making them or repairing them; they are cops and those who avoid the law. A few go to college if and when they can, many don't, and some don't finish high school. They have babies and brothers and sisters. They went to war and came back fine or less than, or didn't. They've lived, and they've died. Sometimes they drink too much beer. They've married and divorced and had children who had children. They talk to each other a lot, or a lot about each other. Many know each other's families and histories. And here's this, above all this: Like the bilingual book *Estampas** itself, these are a people who speak two languages at once. Some are better at one than the other, some equally good in the two, but all listen and deal in both. The naïve might want to say they are in two cultures. But

---

* It has to be said that Hinojosa's Spanish, from its castellano to tejano, is not just perfect but beautifully composed on the page. Both high and low, formal and colloquial, his characters speak it as it is heard and used. Which is to say, not always in grammar books. Hinojosa, equally fluent and refined in English, is known to write his books first in Spanish. Only later did he take on the task of translating himself, too, virtually rewriting the pages for the English language versions. The earlier English translations not by him, in a corny drawl and sanitized as if by an overly cautious schoolmarm, sometimes make for awkward reading.

this community is one, undivided, uniquely on this side of the border, going on, year upon year, utterly on its own. That it does so unseen in the United States of America . . . *Bueno*, that's how it is, how it's always been, *ni modo*.

• • •

Mexican American people come from a well-known region of the United States, and yet somehow they are the very least recognized in it. Let me divide the continental United States into five areas we all accept: The Northeast, the Midwest, and the Northwest make up the northern half. In the southern half we have, on the right, the South. There we reckon with a huge area of America's history, the source of the Civil War. There are two sets of people who live there. They are Black, and they are White. Much aware of each other historically, even now African Americans would see its history as African American, with heroes and martyrs of the two hundred years of racial division that put them there. Anglo Americans, on the other hand, still see a past that is predominantly about themselves, the pride and shame of the history of the South, the changes they were forced to accept. Yet both are extremely aware of one another and accept that this is what defines them. To all and any, that is a region of both Black and White. A similar bifurcation might be said of the Southwest region, what was historically New Spain and later Mexico, until, through wars and annexation, it was decreed that its residents were citizens of the US. Naturally there would be Brown people, those of Mexican descent, and there would be White people, those who came to the hungrily expanding United States. And yet, when Americans think of the Southwest—north from the southern half of California, Arizona, New Mexico, the southern regions of Nevada and Colorado and across half of Texas; from the south, the border from Chula Vista–Tijuana to Brownsville-Matamoros—what does anyone hear of Mexican American history and culture that isn't only an Anglicized version of it? Better said, how many people, when they think of the Southwest, think of Mexican Americans naturally living in it? Instead of a Brown-and-White culture, it is a *Blank*-and-White one.

Not to say that the blank isn't filled. There are mounds of stereotypes and caricatures to choose from, clichés as glaring as gapped teeth, bandoliered bandidos, moustached mice with sombreros de charro, to hoarse chihuahuas selling chain food tacos. Even now, in El Paso, a business group from outside the city named its new Triple A baseball team the Chihuahuas. Though not because of the little old city ladies who love them, nor did that patronizing name occur to the owners from their deep knowledge of the dog's non-cartoon origin, simply that it seemed to them as well-established cute and harmless—as ethnically recognizable as a movie Mexican accent—and not strong or fierce for the huge MexAm city. Imagine what could be picked for a team in Birmingham, Alabama, or an Asian American one for Chinatown, San Francisco. Mexican Americans have been powerless (read: too poor) to fight being treated as so insignificant and lesser than in virtually every category. Even the current word "Latino" has come with a marginalization that proportionally elevates the East Coast Latino—Cuban, Dominican, and Puerto Rican—above the MexAm, despite centuries in the American Southwest, despite the fact that inside the demographic it is three to one. In the booming West, that new voting demographic is closer to 90 percent. Yet when the news media questions each group, what is the subject for our Belken County residents? Immigration. Recently in Austin, the fiftieth anniversary celebration of the signing of the 1964 Civil Rights Act was held at the LBJ School of Public Policy. Four living American presidents came to speak. On the light day opening of the event, the Tuesday, the conference's first afternoon panel featured and was led by Julián Castro, the mayor of San Antonio, and Antonio Villaraigosa, former mayor of Los Angeles. The topic? Both born, raised, and educated in the United States, these Belken County Chicanos had become experts on immigration. The implicit understanding is the usual: Always recent immigrants, Mexican Americans are not ever really from here.

The idea that Mexican Americans are foreigners, not long-residing American citizens of American soil, is not in the realm of consideration in the pages of Hinojosa. As aware citizens of Klail, they may discuss relatives in Mexico, but only in the same fashion that other Texans elsewhere might relatives in Louisiana or Kentucky. People in the Valley often talk about San Antonio and Austin, the big cities to the north. Two major characters in Hinojosa's work, Jehú Malacara and Rafa Buenrostro, cousins, are both veterans of the Korean War, have gone to college at the University of Texas, and then have returned to the Valley to engage in business and city politics. Of course they are aware of outside forces, the monied, land-grabbing Anglo Texans who want as much as they can, and then later the drug-monied Mexican nationals who are a new source of Klail City trouble. All this takes up Hinojosa's fiction, along with the domestic travails within—Rafa marrying into a White family, Jehú, a banker working where that money and power is, to Becky Escobar, née Caldwell because of a distant grandparent, who will divorce the jerk Ira Escobar, relearn her lost Spanish, and let the strong, worldly Viola Barragán mentor her . . . and so on, sagas known too well in homes in LA and El Paso and all the rest of the Belken County cities of the US.

Like the ones of these characters, stories such as these are unheard of or ignored outside the county lines. And so it is in the marketplace of literature in its native country. Aside from essayist Richard Rodriguez (beginning with his infamous *Hunger of Memory*), no Mexican American has bypassed the very smallest press markets before a rise to national stature. Rudolfo Anaya's *Bless Me, Ultima* was first published by Quinto Sol Publications in Berkeley, and Sandra Cisneros's *House on Mango Street* was first published by Arte Público Press, now in Houston; both these writers and books came to national prominence, not by the usual acclaim of mainstream books and critics, but by their overwhelming popularity in classrooms, from elementary to high school and then in college and university ethnic studies courses, where there is a natural demand for material that personally involves students—the goal of all education in the humanities. There is a huge Brown demographic growing in the West, in this next America. Yet stories—fiction, nonfiction, poetry—about the residents of Belken are still seldom seen in mainstream books or magazines, virtually never taught in any mainstream courses in American literature, seldom even in Texas or Southwestern lit courses. Though the past few years have opened the very heavy, creaky doors of the vaults, this not-foreign life from Belken County has continued to be little seen and little acknowledged.

From *Estampas*, first published in 1973 at Quinto Sol in Berkeley, to where he is now, twenty-four volumes later, the vast majority with Arte Público, all of Rolando Hinojosa's work has appeared in small presses. He has received little national attention. And yet, hidden in plain sight much like those in Klail, he does not care. Hinojosa, first published over forty years ago, will tell you he did not get into this work thinking it would ching-ching him to those bright lights and that big city known as New York. When I first heard he'd been honored with a lifetime achievement award from the NBCC and wrote him, late, to congratulate him for it, it wasn't until early morning that it reached him. His reply was his usual style, elegant and quirky both, both good morning casual and *gracias* with sincerity. But in the afternoon came another, in a kind of email whisper: "Una pequeña molestia. What do the initials stand for?" I am certain many reading this wondered the same. And why would they, or he, know? The National Book Critics Circle—the NBCC—gives its Ivan Sandrof Lifetime Achievement Award only to book culture institutions as well-known, and often popu-larly obscure, as the Library of Congress, the PEN American Center, and Dalkey Archive Press, to people whose names are equal to institutions of literature, such as William Maxwell, Leslie Fiedler, Pauline Kael, Lawrence Ferlinghetti, Studs Terkel, and Joyce Carol Oates. Hinojosa may not have known what the letters from the acronym stood for, but I bet no one from Belken County, so far from the center of a publishing world, has heard of any of these, its best-known honorees.

• • •

I love the memory of my first visit with Rolando Hinojosa in 1988. It was probably also my first time on the UT campus not as one of the unem-ployed (years earlier I was trying to get a carpenter's job as they started construction on the then "new" student union). I'd knocked on his office door, which was already a crack open. He swiveled around as I came in, then swiveled again to a mini-refrigerator he kept on a file cabinet and where he got us each a bottle of Corona. It was scorching outside, though not so much in Parlin Hall. His office was admirably—for me a writer cliché I aspired to—overstuffed with shelved books and teetering piles of ones not put away. I sat. Like goodbyes, I hate hellos. So I fumbled, went to an obvious: So, who's your favorite Chicano writer? He didn't blink. He swung to his nearest bookwall and drew out a Heinrich Böll. I cracked up. I knew we'd get along.

As I tell him this memory, now some twenty-five years later, I mention not remembering which Böll it was.

Group Portrait with Lady, he quickly says. That makes me smile, new, all over again.

It's the last days of the spring semester at the University of Texas, and Professor Hinojosa, now eighty-two, who has been caught up in his finals and grading them, makes time for us to have lunch. I come with really only one question, about that homing instinct. I knew it had nothing to do with him, his life story, his fiction, or his award. The whole point of this essay is that he's always had that answer.

Where he actually lives now is near the MoPac highway in an older North Austin complex named after a region in France, its sign done up in flamboyant calligraphy. Not yet "hotter than Texas," there are tornado worries to the north of the state. A light mist smears the windshield. I've driven past the front gates to wait by the central pool. Around it are those poled carports for the at least five-years-old and older Toyotas, Hondas, and Fords, only some of which are there, leaving more room to see. I'm supposed to meet him somewhere near here and I'm looking at as many of the two-story buildings with numbers instead of names and strange mansard roofs as I can.

I finally find him under a tree, using it for an umbrella. The plan was to go to a nearby place and, zip zip, we're there, but they're not. Closed. Now it's raining. And humidity not only steams my glasses, it fogs my car's windows from the outside. I have no choice but to roll them down to see out the side mirrors. All of this trouble I've caused! We're in the road maze—auto repairs and parts, discount furniture, strip joints and liquor stores—of what residents speed through as on a highway, me driving slow only in comparison, our new search, without a pissed, huge pickup nuzzling from behind, or a more huge semi roaring whichever roar, the wipers wiping, rain rolling down the inside of my car's doors. When I saw Jefes (not the possessive, the plural!) we both agreed it was it.

I don't think either of us was so hungry. We were relieved it was open and we were out of the car. Inside, it was like we'd dropped in on Mexico, and as its only customers, so many tables, anywhere, we felt like opulent guests. Where's a more perfect north Austin setting—the grumble of a Texas double-wide road right over there—for the First Resident of Belken County and me, a simple citizen?

I had my other questions—about his visits, as a Chicano writer in America, to Spain and Germany (he does speak a little German), about the little visibility of his war years, Korea, paralleling his visibility as a writer (he's most proud of his war poetry), about his early influences (young, he read all the time, everybody in his home did, and in the Valley, it was always in Spanish, and his best friends became writers Tomás Rivera and Américo Paredes)—but the one that mattered most to me was about home: He not only goes back to the Valley often, that very week he'd be giving the commencement address at Mercedes High School, where he himself graduated so many years ago. He's lived in Austin since 1981 when he took a position at UT, and both his daughters live here. Driving himself a few hours to give back, or taking a bus across town to the job he is devoted to, being near those who love him, who he loves . . . what else?

But that can't be a good enough ending! Must be the restaurant wasn't Mexican right because it was too really Mexican, or driving him back to an apartment complex, not some ranch on the Río Bravo, to grade papers? But wait. It'd become a beautiful day when we opened the glass door. The sun was out, the gray sky blued. It wasn't even hot. But no Aztec dancers with shell anklets and headdresses of feathers *de quetzales*. Not mariachis in *trajes de charro*, the trumpets aimed high, the bajo sextos loud and low, the deep clucks of a bass, and a few *gritos* of pride. That would have been nice in Hollywood or even for New York—would've been nice in Austin or in the Rio Grande Valley—but this: don Rolando Hinojosa, calm and steady as always, past all the battles and wars, was still here, right here as he has been for so many, many years, and he is home, as he will be for so many years to come.

WE HAVE BEEN HERE ALL ALONG

Cormac McCarthy may not have noticed Mexican Americans in El Paso, even when they served him coffee and pancakes at the Village Inn or dinner at Luby's Cafeteria . . . bueno, kind of true they weren't writers from wealthy Tennessee.

I ended up in the Southwest because I knew that nobody had ever written about it. Besides Coca-Cola, the other thing that is universally known is cowboys and Indians. You can go to a mountain village in Mongolia and they'll know about cowboys. But nobody had taken it seriously, not in 200 years. I thought, here's a good subject. And it was.
—Cormac McCarthy (*Wall Street Journal*, November 20, 2009)

WE DO NOT EXIST. We who have lived here have not existed for 200 years, and it has taken the Gothic border Romanticism of our most beloved "Southwestern" writer—Cormac McCarthy, of Rhode Island birth and Tennessee upbringing—to remind us yet again how that *frontera* so well used by him has nothing to do with Mexican Americans. Enchiladas in his books are sure savored, and the Spanish which his main characters always drawl so interestingly on the page, in audio and film, he means as exclusive literary patois, too. Nothing to do with the people in that culture around him in the Southwest. This even though Mr. McCarthy lived in El Paso, Texas, that enormous border city maybe 90 percent MexAm. For at least fifteen years he lived there, enjoying a pancake breakfast at the Village Inn restaurant he was fond of, where the waitress serving him was named maybe Yoli, not cowboy, Indian, or Mongolian. True, she probably was not much of a writer or reader.

But really what he's saying is nothing new for us. I'm betting that you didn't think of the Mexican Americans living here either when you read what he said. Happens all the time. It's been happening for . . . well, at least 200 years.

Consider the geography of the American Southwest, the vastness that it is—New Mexico, Arizona, and Southern California. Go ahead and add much of Northern California below San Francisco, and, if not all, at least the southern half of Texas. You thereby have the populated reach of what was once New Spain, or as it became known, Mexico. Imagine those people who lived there as Mexicans and became American citizens by writ, through treaty, years before the Civil War. Watch their families and communities grow. But then watch—this is something going on for a long, long time—its culture, as it expands, mysteriously recede from the view and history of America, becoming a touristy Chinatown at best, as though its people were transplanted from an exotic island, its culture only immigrant, exotic, remote, foreign.

What if you imagined a South without African American people in it. Impossible, right? The South is as much a history of the Black people enslaved as of those who enslaved them. Mississippi, Alabama, Georgia, those are states that dramatize the Black-White of American Civil War history: All about White to many raised there, all about Black to others equally there, while in the east that is Boston, New York, even Washington, DC, those so distant southern regions are viewed even more as a split of the one color and the other, in a yin-yang whirl of racial conflict and compromise.

Imagine seeing the South with its Black culture but not with Black history, a public memory, in it. Visualize the entire region of the South that way, as if the Confederacy won and kept their slaves in place, as it wanted. Or say they didn't win, but they didn't lose either, and time just passed, the issue of African Americans never dealt with directly, the regional economics left, laissez-faire, to take care of itself: Those Black people, would they be *existing* Americans as White Americans are?

Mexican Americans, who do exist, are soon to be 50 percent of the American Southwest. That is, one in every two people. Today when you look into the public classrooms of its largest cities—ones with those foreign-language names of Los Angeles, San Diego, Fresno, Santa Ana, Las Cruces, Albuquerque, Española, El Paso, Laredo, San Antonio, but even the region's ones with no need of italicization, like Phoenix, Tucson, Riverside, McAllen, Houston, Dallas, Corpus Christi—it would strike you that it might be far more than 50 percent right now. For many years—and even now—when educated people discuss, for example, the literature of the American South, the names that come up are Faulkner, Penn Warren, Welty, Capote, Porter, Wolfe, Williams, Twain. That invisibility of Black writers in this southern literature is as it is for the Mexican American and its culture done large: When people think of America's spectacular Southwest, when they see the shapes of those states in their mind, it is never about the Brown people who are there. The raw, desolate beauty of the landscape, yes. The hip "Spanish adobe" architecture in it, yes. The tasty food that abides, definitely yes. But the people? Americans know of them like they do a few words of Spanish in Cancún. The people who have lived there, who live there now and still? They are absent, purged, not one pretty shade in that mental map. Legacy, sure, that's very cool. A unique, thriving *living* community and culture? Cowboys and Indians, that's who's there and been there.

Sure, it is true that far away from the West, in the powerful East, "Latino" has become a trendy feature of sidebar journalism pieces that ting like the joyful mambo of Tito Puente. Oddly, as if it too were a southern literature, the Mexican American, at or approaching 70 percent of the entire Latino demographic, is lost there in a full Nuyorican *orquesta*. It's as though Puerto Ricans, Cubans, Dominicans, even Guatemalans and Salvadorans, have not only a proportional population but comparable ties to the mainland of the United States and US history. Even when the intention is to focus, MexAms become distorted into Mexican nationals whose dominant language is Spanish, whose culture is not the border but south of. That is, not those whose story is as embedded in Southwestern American culture as cowboys and ranches, tacos and burritos.

One in every two existing people will be Mexican American in Texas, Arizona, New Mexico—and Southern California is not far behind. Also existing in graphic numbers in the rest of the West, and not to mention in the Midwest that is Illinois, Kansas, Iowa, Wisconsin, Nebraska. And in the South, in Georgia, North Carolina, and Tennessee. And even in the East that is Boston and New York. All the way over to Rhode Island, I'm saying some visible people named Renee and Ysenia are serving huevos rancheros right now.

REMEMBERING THE ALAMO

Even though we try to ignore what is at the foundation of a calumnious myth of Texas, we can't stop the draw of the coonskin hat and Bowie knife.

"S.A. SEES STARS" WAS the headline of the *San Antonio Express-News*. The big, center-of-the-page photo featured Billy Bob Thornton—Davy Crockett in the movie *The Alamo*—smiling for local paparazzi near the walls of the historic Alamo mission. There was a smaller photo at the bottom of the page, a fourth the size, of *raza* behind barriers at the Majestic Theater, site of the premiere, pens and paper waving, mouths open in a plea for autographs. These were the ones seeing stars. Not the ones that twinkle after you've been slapped and punched a few times. That's just how I read it. I haven't seen the movie. I want to I guess, but not for the reason many will, especially Texans, whose almost nationalistic interest parallels a fundamentalist Christian's going to *The Passion of the Christ*. (I can only imagine how uncomfortable, even defensive, Jewish people would feel about going or not going to see that.)

If *The Alamo* were only a western, John Wayne on TNT, the epic big-screen battles and adventures. I miss westerns (which I also hate, but that's another essay). It's not, though. For Chicanos, Mexican Americans, the Alamo, even at its best, is about *them*, about how heroic *they* are, in the land where we both still live. And not just there, that battle. Their kind, our kind. Celebrating the victory against Mexico is, for us, like someone reveling in the story of our drunk, abusive stepfather.

The historical battle over the Alamo was about Mexico defending its national boundaries against North American insurgents, giddy with Manifest Destiny, who decided to make an illegal grab for land. Whether or not it was a romantic blow for Texas liberty, the occupation was an act of disrespect, and the Mexican government, as any country would, sent troops. The mythic story of the Alamo, as it was projected, began when D. W. Griffith, following his *Birth of a Nation* (and its Ku Klux Klan nostalgia), produced *The Martyrs of the Alamo*, where Mexicans were portrayed as archvillains. By the turn of the last century, this account was accepted as the "true" history of the event.

The last time I visited the Alamo was right after Iraq I. Inside the adobe mission, the tour guide choked up with zealous patriotism over the outrageous number of Mexican troops climbing the walls to battle the mission's defenders. I couldn't stop thinking how that approach was what was most praised about America's defeat of Iraq—*that* was some overwhelming force. The Alamo tour guide made those skinny, funny-hatted Mexicans seem dirty, like bandidos who'd ripped off some French uniforms. Sure, it was mentioned here and there that the Mexican army came to defend its territory. But that gets remembered about as well as the Treaty of Guadalupe Hidalgo. You remember that, right?

What does get remembered? Those Mexicans. That in winning a battle, they lost. That they had the audacity to fight. That's also what got remembered as more and more folks from Kentucky and Tennessee, Arkansas and Louisiana, colonized Texas: Mexicans were bad and should go "home," even though home was where they already were. These new immigrants from the north, the kin of Crockett and Bowie, and the law they created for themselves, didn't like or trust these Spanish-speaking Mexicans.

On the back of the Metro page in the *Express-News* the day after *The Alamo* premiere, there was also an article about a march in honor of César Chávez's birthday. There was a photo there, too, a longer shot of a wide trail of "several thousand people," mostly union members and organizers, activists—and common working people, descendants of the Mexicans who settled the land before the Alamo. The story of Chávez's fight doesn't have the makings of a heroic battle movie. His battle hasn't even ended. He has yet to become a Davy Crockett or Jim Bowie. And so there's no epic movie role for him. Or for us.

I know a Chicana, well into her 30s, who worked as an usher for the premiere of *The Alamo* at the Majestic Theater. She earned her minimum wage walking the richly dressed Houstons and Crocketts and Bowies down the aisle for their celebration. Hard to not, we all still need to remember our Alamos.

HOW BOOKS BOUNCE

For chamaca/os who didn't grow up with books or much of a life around the literary art.

MANY HAVE ASKED ME, *How did you become a writer?* This is one of those ordinary questions that comes at Q&A's, but at me I sometimes catch a snarky or world-weary all-caps emphasis on the *you*. I could snap off a couple of words in defense, but the truth is that I, too, find me a curious representative of literature. Real writers are bred like champion racehorses, the offspring of Seabiscuit and Secretariat. When real writers discuss their careers, they refer back (modestly, of course) to what they published before their double-digit birthdays. They had books at home (that's all I need to say there). The very classiest universities begged them to be undergrads, and while there they briefly thought they might become a molecular chemist or an avant-garde sculptor. Now, modestly, these real writers will say they were probably better at one of those. Whereas, in contrast, I read my first book when I was seventeen because, in a less than advanced English class for us special few (I worked a full-time grave-yard shift job as a janitor), one day the teacher mentioned a novel hippies were reading. I wanted to know what hippies read because they seemed to have all kinds of easy goings-on that weren't like mine. And nothing in mine included any books. My pre-janitor years I can't say were busy with any poetic forms other than chrome spokes on wheels and girls who didn't read poetry either. Where I came up, balls were as close to books as I got. I bounced them, hit them, threw them, caught them, guarded them, blocked them, kicked them, jump-shot them. They weren't books. Nobody expected me to read them. I didn't. Neither was it suggested that maybe I try an actual volume with unrounded corners, though if anyone had, I would have made it bounce too.

I was not, in other words, born a writer. And then I went to a junior college. Much of that incentive was not so much improving my brains as not losing them, or my legs, walking point in Vietnam (older friends, drafted, came back not doing great). My first freshman comp paper I got a D. The teacher told me she was being generous. When I failed the class, I was smart enough to know who took night classes—on the curve with the most tired day-job students (mine was full-time too, a department store stock boy), this time, at a lesser community college, I got a B. I did not consider a major in chemistry. The only sculpture I knew of came from Mexico, which, cool-looking and deep, I couldn't say I understood any better than what was taught in art history (nothing Mexican, indigenous, colonial, or modern). I tried a business law class. I liked math but too much homework. Sociology, Political Science, Geography, History, Philosophy—each offered original news to me. I was learning. Excited, I began eating it all up. Though I still feared English. That second semester requirement, when you study literature, I remember having to look up a word in virtually every sentence of Melville's *Billy Budd*. Supposedly American, I thought it had to be from a foreign language, and I wasn't sure if I understood what exactly happened to Mr. Budd. I took the teacher at his word for the explanation of it. Great story!

Oh, how I then fell in love. In the beginning it was any books I called on or which called on me. Books stacked and piled and neatly lined up in rows, new or used or checked out (I even stole them, yes, I here confess!). There were the small ones forgotten in quirky, cramped bottom corners, and ones that took tall ladders to touch, and ones that saw so little light their covers seemed to have recast inward—I loved them the most, these difficult ones, hard to get to know, to understand, odd, too quiet, and bashful, secret. When suddenly I became furtive: Though I would never take a lit class again, I was reading novels and poetry.

How did I become a writer? Something happened, that's pretty clear. Did lightning and thunder burst and blow the ears' hearing, override memory and alter the brain? Am I the product of some secret government experiment that maybe went wrong? How did a boy who cared only about sports—what little reading I would do young was from a newspaper sports page—become a man who would idealize books like classic teams and then become one of its professional "athletes"?

I've always been obsessed with story. Whether it's nature or nurture, or what I like to call my genetic mess, I cannot recall a time when I wasn't listening to a story being told. Father of German descent, he was born in Kentucky but came to Los Angeles young. Mother baptized in Mexico City at the Basilica de Guadalupe. Father joined the Marines to fight the Japanese after Pearl Harbor. She kept the rising sun flag he'd captured as an advance scout. Older, he watched my mother growing up next door to the industrial laundry where he started working when he was thirteen, where she eventually worked too as a teenager (not for long). She grew up in that house next door with her mother, who was my grandmother, who was the mistress of the owner of the laundry who owned the house (what in Spanish is known as *la casa chica*). My grandmother came to the United States after her husband, my grandfather, was killed. By knife, went the story, and in the back. I saw that as literal, not metaphorical. My grandmother came to the United States following her sister, my great-aunt, whose mother had been married at fourteen to a man in his sixties and she had . . . not sure how many but a number of children by him. When my great-aunt turned eighteen, her mother traveled from Xalapa and in the capital rented, with almost all their money, the finest limousine for a visit to the presidential palace. And thus, my great-aunt represented Mexico on a tour to Europe and the United States as an opera singer. She wound up in Hollywood, a

"Mexican" for extra movie work, married to a minor French director. My grandmother died young, making my mother closer to my great-aunt. By the time I am old enough to first see her—old, a widow for years, hard for a young person to imagine any glamorous youth attaching to her—she is nothing but a seamstress who needed money, a job, one of fifty at the industrial laundry where, of course, my father had become the floor boss. She repaired the elastic on bras, my father, bitter by divorce and who knows, enjoyed pointing out. He gave me a job there when I too turned thirteen. And this was when I begin to have my own stories.

When I think about being a writer now, I can't help but think of the improbable travel that my genes have made to get here. This journey. And to think we *each* have one, no matter to what breeding or privilege we were born. Why we perk up to listen, why we are driven to, I have no idea. It's so fun to bounce books on your ride—it's a necessary skill. But go, get out there, and what I know is you'll meet people, you'll see places, you'll hear stories that only you will be able to tell.

TOMATO POTATOE,
CHALUPA SHALOOPA

Taco Bell cuisine! After the franchise's advertising success with an accented Chihuahua doggie (probably not from Mexico, btw, unlike the Xolo), it decided to reinvent the chalupa in an American fast-food way.

LET ME DESCRIBE PLATE #3 at every local Authentic Mexican Restaurant fifty years ago. Imagine an oval, particularly thick ceramic plate being hustled over straight out of an oven, so extremely hot it can only be delivered with a potholder and a warning to never ever touch—it's a hot, hot plate each recipient, individually, will be uniquely told—that is set down a distance from the edge of the table so it won't burn chest hairs, or worse, and the clothes in between. The refried beans are gurgling and the "Spanish" rice is reconstituting into its dry grain state, each welded to another, the peas and carrot chunks mutating away from the vegetable category, and the red sauce of the enchiladas is bubbling like straight lava, the yellow and white cheese topping still sizzling from being on the verge of burning. Wait long enough so the plate can be handled. Then, go on, tip it sideways. Tip it upside down. Toss it to practice dexterity, letting it roll over and over, and catch it. Spin it on a finger like a top, food side down, or roll it on its edge across a long banquet table. Yes, the tablespoon of shredded iceberg lettuce and that thin, very thin slice of a too-green red tomato—colorful garnish—that nobody ever eats anyway, both of them wilted and dehydrated, will fall off. But the rest? Nope. It's a Mexican Frisbee!

The Mexican plate #3 was—and of course still *is* more often than not—what Americans were served at Mexican restaurants miles north of the entire stretch of the border: Tortillas or masa fried or soaked into lots of heavy oil or kneaded in lard, the least expensive ground chuck beef, fatty colored cheese that packages in huge, discount blocks. It is this food that Glen Bell, World War II Marine Corps veteran and owner of Bell's Drive-In hot-dog stand, ate and loved and riffed on until, in San Bernardino, Redlands, and Riverside, the desert, agricultural region of Southern California, he established the first three fast-food taco stands featuring Mexican food, Taco Tia, the concept that was eventually transformed into the mega-chain all America knows for its ad slogans "Run for the Border" and the "*Yo quiero Taco Bell*" Chihuahua dog, not to mention those famed crackly tacos.

I remember when I first encountered what might be called hippie "fusion" Mexican food. I was in Isla Vista, California, a university community where a Bank of America was burned in a student riot that brought out the National Guard in 1970, an era and community where Mr. Kinko opened his first copy shop and that incubated the health and organic food rebellion, believing both would lead to the political contrary of what are now corporate enterprises. For someone like me who'd been raised in the big city, near rainbow-streaked inky pools left from leaking oil pans, distracted by moonlit twinkles of broken half-pints and beer bottles smashed against a curb, the only green growth I really thought about was always in someone else's wallet. In Isla Vista, I saw lettuce and kale and collard grow in public hippie gardens. I was taught how to cut off fresh broccoli and I learned to cook it too. I even got used to cauliflower if it had a good cheese sauce on it. But I sincerely thought things were going way too wacky when I went to an IV Mexican restaurant that had the bizarre cultural audacity to put alfalfa sprouts in a burrito. I grew up, for example, loving Chinese food, though not really those bean sprouts, but I didn't complain when I ate them—you just put enough soy and hot sauce over it all. But alfalfa sprouts in a burrito? *¡N'hombre, qué pinche desmadre!*

Until I started liking it. And then I began to like the idea of it. I liked, for example, the idea of frijoles without that yummy bacon fat that was saved in the coffee can by the sink, or refried days and days after in a scoop or so of Crisco. I was changing with the times too, sure, but I had always loved fresh cooked mushrooms and corn served in butter or lemon, and avocado raw or mashed, and of course fresh jalapeños and serranos, and there was no store fruit sold or invented—oh yeah, *grown*, on those trees they have somewhere—that I didn't seek out. Where I came up, if you were a guy who made a point of eating that decorative slice of tomato—you know, intentionally and not by accident—there were dudes around that would ask you how hot pink your panties were. I was the kind of tough who'd shake his head at one of those *panzones*, especially if he wasn't too much bigger than me, and reach over and take the slice off his plate too.

Plate #3 is not the national plate of Mexico. Mexican food is diverse, if not one of the most complicated cuisines, competitive with Europe's. Even enchiladas aren't really a lasagna of cheese and *carne picada* and chopped onion wrapped in an oil-sogged tortilla; at its purest an enchilada is, first, dredged in *chile* (hence, "*en chile*," equals *enchilada*), then filled with what amounts to a taste of meat or cheese, which then, traditionally, gets a sprinkle of crumbly white fresh cheese, or queso fresco. Enchiladas and tacos are most often not primary meals. Fish is plentiful because there are ocean coasts on either side of the country. And vegetables, including nopales, and peppers, and squash. One of my favorite tacos was of sweet onions with *rajas de chile* in Matamoros. I love the ceviche both in Ensenada, Baja California, and Echo Park, Los Angeles. I love the huevos rancheros, with extra *chile de árbol* over it, at Lucy's in El Paso. My favorite Mexican restaurant in Austin offers tacos de *espinaca* and *hongo* (spinach and mushrooms), and, I'm sorry, that's not hippie, that's Mexican. I have eaten the best pozole ever in Mexico City, and taquerías there only cook straight off a grill near the sidewalk, no fried or ovened anything.

Mexican food is not, by nature, unhealthy—or not more so than French or even Chinese food is. Yet Taco Bell romanticizes the most fattening character of both popular American and Mexican food—it cannot be only a historical irony that this business symbiotically evolved out of and alongside the hot dog and hamburger culture. (Like Bell's original taco stand, McDonald's Ray Kroc opened his first hamburger stand in San Bernardino, while Bell's early business partner became the cofounder of the Del Taco chain, and Bell's wife is said to have come up with the ungrammatical German name for another friend's fledgling business, Der Wienerschnitzel). I would even go so far as to claim that plate #3 was and is not the most common meal in Mexican American homes, in the same way that chop suey was and is not in Chinese American homes. Inexpensive dishes are often created and eaten in the hungriest, make-the-best-of-it times, and poor people eat poor meals with poor products. But I'd even go a step farther. That the #3—well, maybe #5, with two beef tacos as well, the corn tortillas and the meat inside deep fried—is what Anglos, not Mexicans, identified as Mexican food because the Mexican restaurants catered to them, and their dinner money, as one in San Bernardino did to Mr. Bell.

• • •

But consider what has happened in the most populated Mexican American cities at and near the Texas border—El Paso and San Antonio. El Paso in particular is overwhelmed by fast food and national chain restaurants and virtually nothing else. Even Chico's Tacos is a city institution most adored for its cheap hot dogs, burgers, and french fries, while the Hamburger Inn is known for the best of Sunday menudo—with fresh oregano and dried chile and chopped onion and limes—on any late night. It might be that San Antonio has an equal number of chain food joints, but what has to be like three-fourths of the central city's restaurants are making tacos and seems like the competition is as much about who's the closest to 99¢. Breakfast tacos are always of egg and chorizo or potato or *papas con chorizo* or weenie or ham or country sausage or *machacado*. Lunch tacos can be carne guisada, picadillo, chicharrón, country sausage, beef or chicken fajita, carnitas, lengua, carne asada—okay, one of guacamole, another of beans, but aside from that, and a spoonful of tomato blended for the *salsita de chile*, not a vegetable in the place and there are no fruits for dessert. These are not tacos made with deep-fried corn tortillas. They are handmade on the spot and toasted on a grill and they are flour. They are good. The fluffiness of flour tortillas comes from the manteca. The fluffier they are, the more lard.

Okay, though I do love healthy food, like everyone, I also love fluffy flour tortillas, the same as everyone does chocolate cake. I happen to love lightly fried corn tortillas—sprinkle salt on it while it's still hot, even a little *limón*, and I don't even need a filling. I love french fries fried with chorizo. I love too much cheese. There isn't a taco listed above I don't love to eat. I love fast-food burgers especially if I can layer it with some slices of fresh or marinated jalapeño. I love Polish hot dogs. *Híjole*, I love fried bologna sandwiches with Tapatío hot sauce! I love tamales, green, red, or sweet. But. But, except, the problem is: It's the fluffiness portion again, and "the best" tamales are like 50 percent lard fluffy!

While the filming proceeded on the latest version of *The Alamo* a couple of years ago, the gossip around the Austin movie scene was that there was trouble casting a Mexican army, which, in that other century, was especially hungry—which is to say, slender. I have not checked to see if the gossip was true, but you don't have to be looking for extras to notice. For example, I was in the sweetest hidden-away taco restaurant in San Antonio on a recent Sunday. Decorative tinsel frills of blue, silver, green, gold, and red crisscrossed the ceiling, the walls were lime green, the plastic tablecloths were blue-white, the dark carpet had lavender flowers, the chairs were orange vinyl, and there were probably seventy-five of them, and you had to wait for a table for *lonche*. The only thin person there was a woman maybe ninety years old with a walker. How many breakfast tacos can possibly fit between a tight belt and the memory of a small waist? How many flour tortillas? Let's not play around with it—just look at the schoolyards! Of course the explanation is not that there's such an overabundance of wealth that we feast at a gluttonous Henry VIII banquet table. Some defend the bulk, calling it all a genetic propensity. Probably it is, especially while even that thin slice of tomato is avoided. It's that *lo barato sale caro*. That is, it's poverty, the food of the undereducated and underpaid, unexposed and untraveled, the people who find *tacos de espinaca y hongos* weird and who find, in a taco of *huevos con weenie* and a Texas-sized Coke, the satisfying comfort of home.

• • •

Though it's really meant to be a drive-through experience, I recently spent an hour, 6:00–7:00 p.m., with a *muy* sugary sweet lemonade inside a South Austin Taco Bell. I will say, no offense, it brings on a strange motel-like experience. The music: Elton John, Natalie Merchant, Carly Simon, Bob Seger. The patrons: a hefty, graying, kind-looking White guy with a baseball cap and a mentally disabled Mexican American he clearly took care of, who was probably the same age, give or take. An XXL Black couple. A Chicano gordito alone. A mami, a little heavy, and her cute overweight daughter who went to refill her oil-drum-sized soda cup before they left. A family walked in, or what seemed like one. A Spanish-only-speaking mexicana mom and her three big teenage sons. Only one of the boys was belly-round and soft; the others might just be called big kids. They were laughing, happy, which resonated in the punishing stillness that had been there. Just because that Taco Bell advertising push was driving me insane, as the cashier who sold me my drink, a scrawny White teenager with black-rimmed glasses, came near to pull out the full trash bag and replace it with a new plastic liner, I asked him to tell me what a chalupa was. You see, BTB—that is, Before Taco Bell—I thought I knew what a chalupa looked like, but then I am dumb. He described the meat and the cheese and lettuce and that it was inside a fried shell. I mean, I asked, how's it different from a taco? It's bigger, he said. That *is* exactly how it seems in its beautiful photo-shoot poses: Just like a taco, which beside the big chalupa looks like a little boy, while his daddy is a hefty NFL pro, grown-up. So, I asked, how's the shell different from the taco's shell? It's thicker, he answered.

This South Austin Taco Bell is a compact neighborhood, of very rich, rich, middle, lower middle, poor, and homeless. All the racial cross section and mix is seen here. Sharing the same asphalted area is, on its east, an old-school McDonald's, and on its west a Goodyear Tire and Care Center. Across the street is, among others, a Radio Shack and a Dollar Store and a popular Family Thrift Store, a Rosie's Tamale House (not so great), and a Mandarin Chinese place (kind of too sticky and spooky dark inside to even trust the takeout). It's not more than a couple of blocks away from good Mexican restaurants. La Nueva Onda specializes in breakfast tacos and *fideo* bowls. Curra's serves the best from the interior of Mexico, like *cochinita pibil* and *mixiote*, maintaining the finest tequilas, and it's not that far west to Polvo's, where lots of vegetables come with most *platos*, or from the meat market Moreliana's, where tacos here are like tacos across and the *chile de aguacate* makes both Mexicans and non-Mexicans want to celebrate with a *grito*.

What I'm saying is that when I went into the Taco Bell the next time, for lunch, it was willful. I couldn't remember what one of those tacos tasted like. Like everyone else, I had relented, to be polite to others, once or twice in my teenage years. So long ago, it seemed like before BTB. And here's the truth—I was afraid I would outright like the taco. I mean, I know I shouldn't, but, bad, I sneak a Mega Grab Doritos now and then and I eat too many tortilla chips at Polvo's before I get my favorite fish dinner and I used to really like cheap hamburgers and so how could I not think, if unhealthy like the aforementioned, I wouldn't like a taco that would be a combo of all those with some curls of cheese and ribbons of iceberg lettuce and a few tomato chunks that were now a settled source of a union dispute? I arrived at the same time as a cute, thin Chicana did—I opened the door for her and she ordered first. She was eating there. I say, by her voice, she didn't know Spanish. At my turn I ask this cashier, just to hear his answer, what a chalupa is. This cashier I swear is the same dude at the corner up the street at the highway on-ramp who up and back walks a cardboard sign, "Anything Will Help." He turns and points to the image of a big chalupa on the framed plastic menu. What's in it? I ask. When he starts to read to me, very slowly, the description off the menu, I stop him. I order one chalupa and one taco, to go, and I wait, listening to Norah Jones. At the drive-up window, the young woman with the headsets is talking English comfortably into the mike but switches into a more comfortable Spanish with another employee I can't see, who speaks only Spanish and cooks. A Black woman announces my number, knowing it's mine before I can find first the receipt and then the number on it, winking, and I grab a handful of the "Fire" packets of hot sauce and throw them into the "Spice Up the Night" bag and set myself up once I get home.

How's a Taco Bell chalupa not like a Taco Bell taco? It is a lot bigger, maybe by two. The beef one I bought had sour cream in it. But the shell, well, it is not corn like the taco's but is a thick, white-flour pita bread that has been fried on the outside so that it keeps its U shape but isn't hard inside. The main filling in both was the meat, the beef, what would be picadillo on a Mexican food menu. I ate them both, and let me tell you unvaguely, directly reflecting the complete and utter surprise that I myself did not anticipate, how genuinely awful the meat was. Spiced, if you'll excuse the expression, somewhere between very lousy chili and the worst jar of spaghetti meat sauce only a lot less good. It was so bad it doesn't even matter for me to say I didn't like the taste of that chalupa shell much or that the taco's shell wasn't nearly as good as the cheapest generic grocery store tortilla chips, because those are complaints along the lines of griping that Walmart doesn't have a fine enough selection of clothing. I won't even bother to be polite and say that I liked the sour cream, you know, to think of something nice to say. Because it doesn't matter. Both the chalupa and taco were so sincerely awful, a food thinking so outside the buns, that I can't even praise the few chunks of tasteless, if still possibly a little healthy, tomato.

...

But putting that all aside—I know, but putting all that aside anyway—
there is something uniquely American happening because of the Taco Bell
phenomenon. The people working there describe exactly the diversity of
the American culture, a workplace where a Mexican national who speaks
English poorly works with a nerdy White kid and a honey-talking Black
woman, where the manager, with two young children, might be named Jim
or Ernesto or Tamiqua. And so what if this food's no more Mexican than
a Big Mac is from Hamburg, Germany—lots of people think it is, and if
they think they like Mexican food, and then they want to try tacos at real
Mexican restaurants, they may learn that they like not only the food but
Mexican people and Mexican culture. That is not how it has been in even the
recent past. It represents a positive when other American people might come
to understand how *American* Mexican Americans are—seeing that mom
and her three sons talking, laughing, eating the same bad chalupas as they do
and not knowing any better. It's an Oprah's Book Club bringing culture to
the dinner table—okay, so maybe to the coffee table in front of the tube, or
maybe through the driver's window and spilled onto the car seat.

Taco Bell's seasoned ground meat isn't picadillo because it isn't
Mexican. The taco, and its filling, is American now. Like spaghetti that
really isn't very Italian, like potatoes that are not only for the Irish, like
french bread isn't French, like a kosher dill pickle isn't only Jewish anymore, a taco from Taco Bell is what food from Mexico can never become
because of its variation and specialties in different regions not only on the
other side of the border, but even on this, the American side: Burritos, huge
in popularity and girth in California, are exotic in borderlands Texas and
New Mexico, while breakfast tacos, craved by all who live in a city like San
Antonio, go virtually unheard of from El Paso to Los Angeles. Taco Bell's
non- or pan-regional taco crosses every state line, and carries across the
country an idea, if not the reality, of an American culture that comes from
Mexico.

It is, in other words, an American food. Tacos in those crackable mass-produced shells (which Mr. Glen Bell claims to have pioneered, if not patented) purchasable in sealed, airtight plastic, sold in grocery stores in Maine or Montana, are now no more ethnic than pizza, or a submarine sandwich.

Tacos are as everywhere as hamburgers and hot dogs, hot & sour and soy sauce, ketchup and salsa. This is an American taco born into a culture without any relatives in Mexico or in the borderlands anymore, a culture that mispronounces a few words in Spanish the same as it does a couple in Italian or Greek or German.

And Taco Bell's success is not only as an implosion of a not very healthy glop, but has to have been the commercial inspiration to at least two new regional fast-food chains—Taco Cabana from Texas and Baja Fresh from California—which dare to feature what would have once-upon-a-time been a foreign, *Mexican* Mexican taco. And that fusion of Mexican culture and the healthy hippie—which bloomed sunflower-big into a demand for a nouveau gourmet—is transforming the architecture of food in the Southwest and Texas. In Austin, for instance, where Bush lost big-time in 2004, menus posted outside chic restaurants bear Mexican dish names as stylized as if they were French or Italian influenced. And what was unheard of when Mr. Bell first ate plate #3, Mexican restaurants themselves, owned by Mexican immigrants who stay near the cash registers and in the kitchens, no longer look to hire petite waitresses from Tamaulipas or Monterrey, but tattooed, slacker-hip White dudes who wear ball caps and cool T-shirts and say "dude" at various times as part of their personalized service.

One last thing, just for the record. That freaking "chalupa" is not a *chalupa*! The word "chalupa," like the word "taco," draws up a specific, historical image—more like a tostada than a taco, but with a canoe-like rim on it—and it's one that does not look like a taco any more than it does a chili dog or a steak sandwich. If any old Mexican word can be attached to Taco Bell's latest creation, they might as well call it an enchilada. Enough of the customers won't know any different, most won't care, and in time restaurants will have to explain what those items on a plate that used to be called enchiladas are. Since this chalupa doesn't have Mexican corn in it, why not name it after a Spanish dish, like paella, an exotic name, or, like a car, give it the name of a famous Spanish city, like Toledo, maybe with a little vowel variation on it, so it might be called a Tolido Taco. Or take it on like Mrs. Bell would. Something like La Taco Perro.

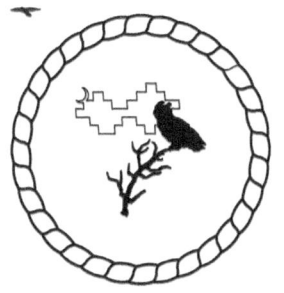

NOW YOU DON'T SEE US, STILL YOU DON'T

It has to end, please.

LIKE FRIDA KAHLO, I was born in a split screen—in Mexican America, my mother's side, where I lived with my mom who was proud of who she was and where she came from, and what I call my father's, with whom I never lived, a German American who grew up beside Mexicans, whose ability in Spanish at his job made him the image of a boss. He taught me one big secret . . . call it his unflorid American *dicho*: "Never tell anyone you're Mexican, say you're Spanish." Thoughtful, early '60s socioeconomic advice? Kind of a strange thing for him to tell me. Many years later I figured out he was likely pissed off, even wounded, because my mom didn't want to be married to him.

My mom often got all kinds of nasty assumptions pushed into her because she was a "Latin" woman—the polite euphemism of then, like Negro. When I was young, she was also a divorcée. That and her seductive, hot Latin powers upset married men so much, I wasn't allowed to be friends with certain kids—by their parents—kids I'd meet at schools or on teams. Kids from good homes, as they say. And there were equally silly things, inoffensive, just dumb. For example, Mexican women, all of them, were born cooking, meaning like in a Mexican restaurant. Tacos, enchiladas, and not bologna sandwiches I made for myself. (I put green chile or jalapeños in them.) My mom was out most of the time, at work in the daytime, drinking and on dates at night. Never home, seldom cooking, never enchiladas. And yet, if anyone came over, and the conversation went there, she too felt obliged to commit to her genetic inheritance. She did open cans well once in a while. Those tops of salsas red or green could peel right off.

Then there's me. That's gone on a while. I'm male. Which *means*. I probably do watch more basketball on TV than most women—and also yes, I am heterosexual. I'm guilty of all, and there it is, proven: *Latin* blood, *macho*! This despite exculpatory facts about me. The complexity of each of us, not the simplicity of "All men are panting dogs," or "All women are conniving bitches," and so on with mass ethnic etcetera generalizations. Like, despite my howling and whoring testosterone, I studied religion in college, my major and grad degree. Ideals, the platonic heights, not money, scores, and gains—not finance, fame, or power. I can make an international list of hit mystics I read silently, peacefully, ones I, if you'll excuse the expression when it comes to macho me, "studied." I guess not enough to counterbalance a cliché's hormones. And thus it is that when I tell people I am so guilty of being a brute *culo* that I forced my wife to have two sons, too many ponder instead of laugh.

In the late '80s I came to Austin, which for me was the South, as far east as I'd ever been. A magazine editor took me to a nice restaurant for lunch. And, wild me, I talked to a busboy who was Mexican. Asked him where he was from and a couple things like that. The editor was shocked, but also fascinated. Had he never seen a person like this converse at a table he was at? Never noticed these workers, these people, realized they spoke in normal voices? Dark, they'd be called *indios* in earlier centuries, *indígenas* now. The editor was like a Spaniard on a new journey to a land where he already lived. I was more than surprised to learn that not only didn't so many people know there were Mexicans in their daily world, but that *mexicanos* had human lives like theirs.

The world of my father's screen side often sees everything I've done as generated from below my belt, not above my shoulders. I can't tell you how many times I've been told I was smart, as remarkable a surprise to those who discover this in me as to a New York literary agent impressed that I spoke English okay. I'm not telling *you* I am so smart, only that I'm not really only *Latin* juices. Nobody ever thought writer Norman Mailer, proud to be a pugilistic man's man, often little more than fists with his notches of women, wasn't smart, but I'd suggest that because he was New York and Jewish, his maleness was considered an intellectual stance—how he thought of it too—not something his people are born with.

A few years ago, I was interviewed by a *Texas Monthly* journalist because I had a new book, *Before the End, After the Beginning*. When the piece came out in *The New York Times* as a profile, the writer claimed I'd described myself as, quote, "brawny and strong," unquote. That is, I had supposedly chosen those two synonymous words, and both came from my own mouth. *Brawny?* That word? The paper towel dude, the lumberjack? I certainly would have chosen two adjectives that contrast—*contrast*, as opposed to meaning the same thing. Dumb enough I guess, stunned, it took me three weeks to finally figure out what I'd actually said: Asked how my work is described, I'd come up with not brawny, but *brainy* and strong. That is, I once was a high-rise construction worker who was also educated—as in, I have a master's degree, right?—and now I am a writer who is physically messed up—disabled. I was still suffering the consequences of a recent brain injury, and I still slurred words. (How could he mishear a word I'd never use?) From his other world, how could that journalist hear me say "brainy" when he believed I live off juices that rage way way beneath my Chicano head?

That other world has its views of us in their history. Of course I could go on at length on this topic of, according to their firm beliefs of faith, how little Mexico and Mexican culture are valued in the world—and not only in this huge southwestern quadrant of the United States, but in the entire country. For instance, think of the state in the union most American, its true "back home." One that reflects the most nostalgic image America has of its lush bounty, where all presidential candidates must go to begin the election cycle. And what is Iowa famous for? What is that crop that is the most fresh, healthy icon of American virtue and wholesomeness? Corn, yellow as the sun on a spring day. It is in the cornfields where Kevin Costner builds his field of dreams. Oh so American roots romantic! *Bueno,* sorry, you may be a little surprised, but it so happens that corn is the most indigenous, ancient product of Mexico—central México exactly, the first seeds there and by sacred cultivation and meticulous cross-pollination over many centuries. Where corn *was* God, was worshipped as a god, where working the *milpas* was what people did, and corn, as tortilla, was what all people were made of.

Another: I learned that "chili"—LA's TV Detective Columbo's favorite dish—isn't Mexican, it's Texan, American. It says this in a major history of cuisine. Though it is true, I read, that it seems to be like a similar dish found especially in northern Mexico. Around this part of where we are, in El Paso, what was once called northern Mexico, the dish would be called frijoles. In restaurants called Mexican these days, they're charro or borracho beans. It's true that that other world added ketchup and Worcestershire and whatever to theirs, and a lot more meat (because they're richer), and they can even take the beans out. But not the chiles. Those are, excuse me, from Mexican culture. It is true that the *e* was lopped off *chile* for an *i*, so it's like they say it, *chili.* That made it American all the way, nothing at all to do with Mexicans.

When I used to coach here in El Paso (nine years I did that), the kids would eat popcorn and potato chips and all sort of unhealthy crap. What did they soak all that in? Louisiana. And maybe in Louisiana and much of the US and even here in El Paso, among our own children and a few parents, they might believe that a chile sauce which you see everywhere in México originated in Louisiana. . . . Or you know Tabasco sauce? How do you suppose certain very conservative types would react, as they splash it onto their huge steaks, to learn that *tabasco* isn't some strange word for spicy all-American hot sauce? That the word is a state in México, named maybe after the very river that Cortés first traveled when he went into its interior (where and when he was given Malinche as a gift), and is often associated with the native peoples who were living there at the time. In other words, aside from the name, and the chiles, and the history of Mexican sauces all over Mexico and even in the state of Tabasco—where, incidentally, many ships from the port of New Orleans docked to import goods and probably unload slave-picked cotton—Tabasco sauce was invented and made in Louisiana by an Irish-named family and is American.

There may be . . . call them *nefarious* reasons for all this ignore-ance (I like dividing that word into two, Texas-like), but I want to think large, good, deep. Big because this has gone on so long. Like more than one century. Two. And especially after the Mexican-American War was lost. After James K. Polk, pro-slavery Southern president, decided to get the Southwest by any means necessary. We skip all that. See us as larger and wiser and exotic even. So exotic that we're like Chinese sages, every *mexicano* and *chicanito* who has ever been here. One of the greatest philosophers of China, Lao-tzu, wrote one of the most influential books in human history called the *Tao Te Ching*. There is too much in there, but I quote one line: "The perfect sage leaves no tracks." What does this mean? The essence of what came to be called Taoism, a few hours can be spent on this. Here's less: What is the perfect government? Not the one that is messing up, because everyone sees that and complains. No, it is the one proceeding so smoothly that people forget it is there. It leaves, in other words, no tracks, no footprints. It is this way with so many people we count on and not. The perfect gardener leaves the yard looking as though it were nature itself. The perfect thief goes in and out and no one knows the place was violated. The perfect carpenter is one whose doors open and close so seamlessly, whose cuts are so taken for granted, it never occurs to anyone to remark on any of the fine, skilled work done. And thus, say I, are we: So much given, and taken, all done so perfectly, it is simply that there are no footprints to be seen.

RIVERA AND RULFO

This was for an anthology of fifty well known American writers, each choosing two stories by world writers. Neither Rivera or Rulfo are known entities in our country's landscape.

BACK IN THE OLD, old days of American literature—call that pre-1975—not every writer was expected to live and study in the same way. If being smart enough was a baseline, being educated was essential, but that didn't mean a writer was a perfect student, with perfect grades, who went to the perfect schools and got perfect jobs. The writers I loved lived in an outside land that expected engagement—generally that was with the wealthy (even the poor like to read about the much better off), a real adventure with risk, but it could be inside a poor or weekly paycheck community, all of which probably reflected the writer's actual personal life, region, and occupation. Ideas came from inside a day-to-day world, were learned. So different for the American writer of now, who formulates ideas and researches material from a library or its equivalent, the stories shaped from inside the head, not by experience and surprise. I've even noted that a writer now is "from" a grad school she attended, "from" a program he teaches creative writing in . . . and that's when I hear Pete Seeger:

There's a green one and a pink one
And a blue one and a yellow one
And they're all made out of ticky-tacky,
And they all look just the same.

And the people in the houses . . .
. . . they all get put in boxes
And they all come out the same.

I didn't grow up wanting to become a writer, an aspiration as never heard of as someone wanting to be a governor. In my home and neighborhood there weren't many books or readers of them—any, as far as I knew. But there were a lot of storytellers. Lots of them were liars or scam artists or bullshitters, players and hustlers both male and female, and saps, suckers, and losers, each with stories charged by the unreal in the real, which had consequences that seemed unreal but were too real.

I was so thrilled when—in my twenties—I found out about literature. It became the religion I believed in. The writers I loved were saviors howling in joy or lamentation at inappropriate times, seekers of mysteries and truths whispered privately between the lines. Their characters had lives I recognized, ones who took me home even when it wasn't really very close to where I ever lived. They wrote stories that were more myth tales: They gave me ideas that seemed fresh and new but were, at the same time, ones I already carried deep inside me.

They, characters and writers, were not raised only in family happiness and comfort, and they sometimes chose wrong and worked bad jobs; they met the best people who were in fact sleazes, or the least interesting who were invisible saints. And they came back to tell, to reassure me, their reader, that I too was living a life deeply, not like an oh-so-cool celebrity in the successful birth spotlight, but like the simple, admirable ones who few paid any attention to, who lived commonly and died commonly—remembered only by the myths of the small stories left behind.

Excuse this aside: Lots treat the story as "short," as in junior, and mean it's not as ambitious or important as a novel at the adult table (evidence, that a novel isn't called a "long" story). There are those who'd go after poetry for even being shorter still. A story has a closer kinship to poetry than to novels. A great story, like a great poem, is made huge by its myopic obsession on the small, saying more in the fewest lines, in carefully executed language and scene.

And so many writers and stories I loved, and from so many countries and regions not mine—and probably because they were, it wasn't until I read those from my own mental and visual landscape that I realized what writing might be for me: People I knew, culture I lived in, places I'd been but that the American literature I read didn't acknowledge as existing.

"LA NOCHE BUENA" BY TOMÁS RIVERA

Tomás Rivera's "La Noche Buena," on the surface, would seem to be simply about a very poor provincial mother so trapped by her own agorapho-bia that she's unable to go even a few blocks in a small Texas city to buy Christmas Eve presents for her young sons, who want the American hol-iday. Easy analysis is of the difficult generational transition from Mexican to American, the poverty of these people on the border. But that misses so much. Setting aside the colloquial tejano Spanish used, the literary shock of that itself (in a collection first published bilingually), here was a world unseen in print by the many of us who know the exact house she lives in, who know those tracks she crosses unto such confusion, have even been in that Kress drugstore—and not from the point of view of an Anglo, Larry McMurtry Texas, but as it is to the other half of the residents of the state. What takes a little more to realize is that doña María's love of her children is so great that she is willing to overcome her most humiliating fears to please them. In a sense to lose them, to let them grow up away from what she can—and can't—give them, which is only, ironically, her stability—a home where she stays and takes care of them. That simple woman with an apron, a mother, soon enough a grandmother. And you leave the story, this unsophisticated woman you knew well and left behind, and ask, How right was she? What would history say?

"PASO DEL NORTE" BY JUAN RULFO

It was Juan Rulfo, the finest Mexican master, who made me read fiction as I would poetry—more slowly, like walking a distance on a scorching day. In Rulfo's stories, life, reality, is a hallucination.

Where most writers are consumed by characters, here the land is God, poverty the human condition. Every conversation, every activity, every emotion was affected by and reflected in the chapped, pitiless landscape that is northern Mexico. I have never been able to resist what for me is one of the greatest stories I've ever read, his "Paso del Norte." It is primarily but a conversation between a grown son and his aging father. Broke, the son has nothing left to do but go north to the United States, cross into El Paso, and find any paying work. He is asking his father to care for his small children and his wife until he can take them back. It is a conversation that cannot be good under any circumstance, anywhere, but here it is drawn as brutally unsentimental as possible. And when the son returns, failed, there is the stunning end, with the saddest, fullest, most layered last line ever written.

DOORS IN OLD GUATE

I miss those tortillas the most.

I'M WANTING TO TAKE a picture of a certain carved wooden door, but, techno clumsy and dumb, I'm too awkward to get it together. A tired sedan first pulls into the space ahead of the empty space in front of my view, and then slowly, very slowly, rolls backward. So inch-by-inch that I have plenty of time to believe it will roll out of my sightline eventually. But no. An elderly gentleman gets out and comes around and, taxi style, opens the back door for a more elderly lady. In the front and beside her are bundles of fresh-cut flowers screaming color. They are taking them not through the door I wanted to phone-shoot, but the bland door just to its north, a short walk around the front of the car and over the sidewalk. The flowers, I can tell, aren't occasional. They are entirely for the door's other side, for the everyday interior, decorative for a personal life and for the week, something commonly beautiful, and inexpensive, south of the US border.

I go back to the other side of the narrow street to wait. As I do every other day after my *cafecito y desayuno*, a few doors away I stop for tortillas. This morning, a little early for this, the young woman always there is still brushing clean her comal, prepping. If I can wait, she says, it'll only be a few minutes. This is the first time in the months I've lived in Antigua

Guatemala that she is working with anyone else, and she is animated, talking full-stream in her native language, Kaqchikel, a Maya dialect. All this time around me and maybe another person who happened to be there, she's been a quiet, shy Spanish-speaker. I have talked to her many times, the smallest things I can think of, or maybe if I am curious about something (e.g., I wanted to know if the tortillas were of masa, not *maseca*, and she looked at me, a glint in her eyes, like I was such an *extranjero*, that they grind their corn right there—the curtain behind her) and I like to make her smile. She knows now how many quetzales worth I want without me saying. I always want to—but won't—take a picture. Not of her, though sure. Not for my memory, because it's there, where I prefer it, locked. It's the photographic darkness all around her, black and smoky gray, that puts the focus all on her and the comal beside her. The natural shadow that takes up the very small space that we at the door see. Not in time. She and her friend are in Maya *trajes* and *delantales*, a store apron worn by all *cocineras* from all regions. Like the manic chatter and squall of birds I hear in the morning outside my bedroom window, the rhythmic patting of the balls of masa into tortillas is another of my favorite soundtracks—one of the oldest Indigenous culture traditions, many thousand years, tortillas being made one at a time.

When I first came here, a few years ago, I liked it, its ragged colonial beauty maintained, held up proudly, but it was a little too San Miguel de Allende for me. Seemed over the line about and for tourists, too many Germans and French, too many Americans, pizza, sandwiches, burgers, menus in English. My favorite café is a hang for those learning Spanish, practicing directly with a native speaker. Too easy to fall back on the dominant financial power culture, to get comfortable like you never left it. But I came again, not Defe or Oaxaca. At my café yes you can overhear awful sentences in awful accents, but I've gone past all that. The servers and staff in the restaurant all know me by name and most what I order. I take a tuk tuk there in the morning because I don't want that walk before my *cafecito*, and I now have Julio come and take me there every day. Living in what in the states would be called the barrio—here a city ten minutes away called Jocotenango—Julio reminds me of every Chicano except he's never heard of Tejas, only knows about the *frontera*, the border, from tales.

As I walk home, about forty minutes, by street and sidewalk—hard to call the streets "cobblestone" when these rocks seem way too prominent and jagged, and the sidewalks, maybe not as perilous as those I've walked in Xalapa or Oaxaca, where they can be cliffs, not curbs, are hazardous (especially to those like me for whom walking isn't as mindlessly easy as it once was)—I seldom see any tourists or expats on the streets or in the businesses I pass or visit. Native people in the cheapest world-corporate clothes are about two-thirds, but the rest—and only the women—are in village *trajes*, many head-to-toe ornate, and all are engaged in buying and selling, car and motorcycle parts, appliances, medicine, pastries, fried chicken. There are the women at the corners and against the edges of the sidewalks, their *canastas* of straw or plastic off their heads, selling *aguacates*, *mandarinas*, *jocotes*, *manzanas*, *bananos*, while others with cloth-covered trays of tortillas and tamales or guatemalteco specialties like *chuchitos* or *paches*, sweetened *güisquil* or *camote*. The commerce is not for tourists, and many people come and go in chrome-grilled and bumpered buses, red green brown, as colorful as blankets—"*¡Guateguateguate, guaa-teee!*" or "*¡Vieja, vieja, vii-ey-jaaa!*"

The truths of life are all around me all the way, all the time: On the same streets the crippled and infirm, the vigorous and gentle; the just-born, wrapped and cradled, the extremely old, a little stooped maybe, shopping bag in hand, walking like in mud toward and from; boys and girls and phones and giggles, a teen arm-in-arm with a grandfather.

I turn a corner and ahead of me a young dad, jeans, T-shirt, running shoes, his baseball cap backward, his daughter, three or four, a cute *trajecito de huipil, faja y falda* (top, belt, skirt) and golden sandals, chirping to her grandmother dressed the same, leading them.

I open the tall iron gate where I am living and Silvio is there, like finally I'm back. He can't wait for us to go to another carpenter together. It's that I want a cedar door made that I've designed myself. There are all kinds of shops that do just this sort of thing.

HECHO EN TEJAS

This was written as the introduction for the anthology of the same title. Though the volume's heft was to show the historical literary work of Mexican Texas (somehow overlooked by the state's scholars), the story of a Chicano becoming aware of himself and his life being linked to a longer history that isn't only based on American chain store wrappings and consumption. You may not think you're from México anymore—proof being you obsess on the Cowboys and don't converse in Spanish, don't like soccer or watch fútbol, being born and raised in San Antonio—but that's where all Chicanos start out.

A YOUNG MAN I will call Michael comes up to me. He wants to talk to me because he was in a creative writing class I taught that read a short story he'd submitted which wasn't received very well because it wasn't very good. It was a ghost story. The setting was an old wooden house. He'd created a faceless and colorless cast of characters—two parents, an older boy, and two younger children who all spoke a bland, perfunctory English. The old wooden house was in San Antonio, and he knew it really well. And those characters who lived there were like him, like his family.

In his midtwenties, Michael lives in San Antonio and was born and raised on the westside—that proverbial poorest and toughest and oldest part of town that all cities have. He is already a father and is raising a daughter by himself. He says he has always wanted to be a writer, but he doesn't want his work to be Latino Hispanic Chicano Whatever. He remembers when he read a particular poet in high school, a San Antonio *activista*, and he thought, well, this wasn't what he was or how he lived. For instance, he didn't even have an exotic name. His is Michael, not Miguel. His Spanish is lousy, if lousy could mean so bad he'd never seriously use what little he might know because he'd fear he'd get most of it wrong. His parents speak English, he says, and only one grandparent really can't.

What does Michael look like? *Este güey es muy moreno*, he is very dark. His last name isn't exactly a bland, everyman Smith or Jones either, not a González, Hernández, Rodríguez. It's a name like Zamarripa—no vague descent attached to it. As to ghost stories, I point out to him that they are often set in New England, or Old England, and that's usually because that's where the writer is from. Usually, I explain, writers write about where they are from. And so if he's from San Antonio, and if the story is supposed to be set in San Antonio, and he's Mexican (for those not, that's the internal vernacular for it), wouldn't it be a good idea, even a lot easier. . . . But he's American, he insists. He watches American TV. He doesn't like soccer, and down there, where he's never been, they like soccer, and he likes football. He doesn't know how to be exotic. But, I tell him, he's from the westside. He looks at me like I'm making it complicated. So, I say again, don't you see how that isn't Montana or New York, it isn't San Francisco or Dallas, Marseilles or Pamplona? His life isn't exotic, he insists. So I ask him what kind of work he does. He's a manager at a Pizza Hut. And his crew? Well, they're all from, uh, San Antonio. I'm laughing now because what he doesn't want to say is they are all Brown people there too. He thinks that isn't exotic! He doesn't think he has a *unique* story to tell. That in the historic city of the Alamo, where the Republic of Texas began and the end of Mexico's national sovereignty ended—this very dirt—he who looks not like anyone on the winner's side of that war, he an adult, responsible man who's earning just above minimum wage as a manager at an "Italian" chain pizza joint with minimum-wage employees who have the same story and descent as him, he wants to tell a ghost story about *Americans* who are . . . like *him*.

But consider the core of what Michael believes: That to reflect on his own life, the people he was born from and with and around, that bringing in his immediate landscape, his historical and family heritage, he'd be making "exotic" talk. That's how far away he is from himself and understanding how and why he became a manager at Pizza Hut. It's almost as though he were a Chinese child adopted by a middle-class American family who never detected what others saw or heard what they said about him. That consciousness, political or personal, awareness of history and place would *estrange* him, transform him into someone who wasn't Miguel enough, or too Miguel, or what is that, where does that come from? Or is it simply that he doesn't know, he has never once thought about it before, or has never been told? Then what is this orphan's deprivation?

Where *does* that come from? Why would he defend a ghost story that isn't about Mexican Americans who live in San Antonio in an old wooden house on the poor side of town? Would he be content to raise his daughter on a literature, like his ghost story, that would never be about where she lived, the land and culture she came from, the American stories of her face, her blood? Wouldn't she be a little proud if her own father had published this American story she read? If he had a book of them? And if *este loco* from *el hueso* wrote ghost stories, any stories, set there, and they were read by people in New England and Old England too?

There is a haunting in Texas, and it is the ghost: A *bisabuela* gone prematurely, whose son was married to someone's mother, whose *abuelito*'s daughter was married to a *tía* who was this other's *nieto*. Hard to know which, how, when, why. But: A mournful voice in a song. Shy eyes in a painting. Joy from an avocado-green bedroom and baby-blue dining room. Respect wrapped in a black shawl, patience scratched into a wooden toy trinket, love in a piñata or paper flower, work in polished boots and huge buckles, saddles or beaded car-seat covers, hats of hard plastic or straw. Strength in simple mashed frijoles seasoned with oregano, *ajo, y cebolla*, in a hot flour tortilla puffing up on a cast-iron comal. In the *pico* of fresh serrano chile spooned into a taco and gordita, from a shiver of sweet from a *leche quemada* candy, in the sigh that comes from the first sip of horchata or *agua de jamaica*. Though its descendants do survive in the poor neighborhoods of Texas (also known on a larger scale as the cities of El Paso or San Antonio, as the regions known as the Rio Grande Valley or South Texas), there is too much that feels deprecated, neglected, or ignored by the more financially boastful, self-contained Anglo Texas culture, as though the flesh and blood cultural legacy of this Mexican ghost could be dismissed or replaced, as though so much of it were like housing projects, transitional or residual, an era that was, not is—or transformed into a market niche, pitched as an advertising campaign, a decorating style or motif.

It's the ghost who hoists up Mexican flags in the Rio Grande Valley. People don't always understand that when they come down here. The voice I hear is Jaime Chahin's, the Dean of the School of Applied Arts at Texas State University. He worked the fields with his family when he was very young, and when he talks of the North, to the east it's Minnesota and to the west it's Washington. When he talks about Idaho, what he can't help talking about most is *el cinturón del diablo*, the devil's belt, which, he says, could hold 100 pounds of potatoes on either side. He is driving me and two dons of Chicano literature, Arturo Madrid and Rolando Hinojosa, and we are on the road to pay respects to the memory of Tomás Rivera, traveling to his birthplace and grave in Crystal City. The ghost is in every conversation and every silence, even when we've pulled up to a country restaurant with little more than a few tables and chairs and its 8x10 black-and-white publicity photo of the singer Rosita Fernández that's been on the wall . . . a long time. Even when we talk about breakfast tacos and a particular meat inside, how in El Paso it's called *machaca* and here it's *machacado*, or how in Los Angeles or Mexico City, what would be *chilaquiles* there might be called *migas* here. When we leave, full, the conversation is of the land and people who are still here or gone or passed on, the children of and their children, about each change and what doesn't seem to ever change, and it is because of the ghost. The ghost both sanctifies and celebrates the gossip about him or her, some whose deeds have gone beyond or some whose legends are local, even ordinary—like a certain Vidal who sold whiskey and was found dead in a motel from an *infarto* because he was with a twenty-two-year-old woman, his corpse gotten out of there by the sheriff fast so his good wife would never know. About a George who flipped out one day and shot cows with an M-16. Or . . . but I have looked out the window over there. Two mesquite trees, dark as shadows, on top of a brown grass lomita, no prickly pear near, no other brush, like it's a prop only missing a horse. It's a Texas photo that only someone from Texas would recognize.

Many say that what would be called *el movimiento* began in Crystal City when, in 1963, a group of five Texas Mexicans, empowered by union organization at the Del Monte canning plant, ran for city council and won in a city, like the entire region and state, where government was run by an Anglo minority. And it was Crystal City again in 1969, when high school students walked out and boycotted to demand more than only one Mexican American cheerleader, and bilingual and bicultural education, and simply more institutional respect of the Brown people who lived their lives there now and historically. The success of this fight launched the first Chicano political party, La Raza Unida, led by José Ángel Gutiérrez, which eventually won electoral control of both the city council and school board.

It is all this that the drive leads us toward, except I am distracted, my eyes looking out the car window but seeing somewhere else. Crystal City has, strangely, my own life in it too. For instance, sure, yes, it is that spinach is my favorite vegetable, and Cristal is the "Spinach Capital of the World," and the city's center even honors Popeye with a statue there, and so I think not only of health but strength (and also I studied philosophy, and Descartes, and we the initiated know the unavoidable depth of Popeye's wisdom: I yam what I yam). But watch—once I had a girlfriend I met at UC Santa Barbara, where we both went to college. She was from Eagle Pass. And because we were young, not sure much of anything, she took a long bus ride home to Texas and soon took a job at Crystal City High. I went to El Paso, driving her car across three deserts to eventually bring it to her, blowing out its head gasket, fixing it, and thereby having maybe $30 left, so that I began living in the cheapest hotels, and finally a YMCA for longer than I want to say. She visited me in El Paso once on a weekend and after that she told me she was pregnant. I would marry her and we would be happy for so many years, love so much the sons we raised together. On that same weekend she brought me a book, *Estampas del valle y otras obras* by Rolando

Hinojosa-S. It could be she had borrowed the book without checking it out, because it was stamped *Crystal City High School Lib.* Probably another good explanation. *Estampas* wasn't only important to me because she gave it to me as a gift, was what she thought I should and would like to read about a region of Texas I only knew through her, but because I was ravenous about books then, and I was only then beginning my want to write, and I wasn't sure of so much about what it was I was doing, what writing was, and, like Michael, I was messed up about who I was, where I came from and belonged. I'd already devoured French and German literature, any dime-store or otherwise paperback Western novel with American Indians as lead characters, especially half-breeds. I read Beat and Grove Press literature, Octavio Paz and Juan Rulfo and the Latin American boom writers. I loved James Baldwin and Langston Hughes, but Richard Wright, he was God. Chicano literature had just begun, and I knew it only through the plays of Luis Valdez, his Teatro Campesino, and the *pachangas* at Casa de la Raza in Santa Barbara. Those were days when to me Chicano meant someone who was involved with the United Farm Workers and César Chávez, and I had come from the city, from Los Angeles, where adults I knew drove beer and delivery trucks, were butchers, office and shipping and sales clerks, plumbers, firemen, repairmen, secretaries, assemblers, mechanics, taxi drivers. I myself had worked so many jobs already—industrial ones, in factories, both union and not—from early in high school on. Unlike all my big city friends, I liked to eat tomatoes and spinach, but I didn't really have a clue about what it meant to work in the fields, and so that was yet another reason I felt separated from *el movimiento* that surrounded me, the one who was reading books about philosophy and religion. If Valdez was creating a Califas of archetypes (and sometimes stereotypes), of hip zoot suiters and lowriders, pachucos *y las rucas*, characters I enjoyed but didn't feel were like me and my more conflicted and ordinary American experience, what I found in Hinojosa's work bled a vein: He was writing about the common people who were cops or menial bank workers, employed at drugstores or who sold cars, went to little league baseball games and told stories of a living Mexico and the smallest *cositas* of a local community, like death and birth, who married who inside the community and out, much of it related as gossip and through simple conversation in dialogue. It was, in other words, what I recognized, and so, like much else that suddenly changed in my life from that point on, I began to understand the world I was in too, where I was not only as a working man, but as a writer I wanted to be.

The writer I am now who is still on such a wondrous, surprising journey—mysterious both in psychic and real space—today I am driving in a car, three decades later, with that book's very Rolando Hinojosa, who I now think of as a friend even, and we are on the road to visit the grave of one of the other legends of Chicano literature, Tomás Rivera.

Which is to say, there is such a tombstone now of our first Chicano writer, and it is, justly, in Crystal City, Texas, in the Benito Juárez Cemetery, where, sure, a few wooden crosses have fallen, but where many stand tagged with tattered blue ribbons or torn, miniature American flags, but where everywhere are cement Virgins, vases of fresh pink roses, petals of paper flowers that are purple and red. Names—Rosalva, Estanislado, Euluteria, or Mariana, Ignacio, Juan, Pedro, Beatriz. Rivera's gravestone is pink granite, probably the same quarry rock that makes the Texas Capitol so admired, RIVERA engraved above the inscriptions, Florencio M, Nov. 7, 1903 to Dec. 5, 1959, his father, and then his, Dr. Tomas H, Dec. 22, 1935 to May 16, 1984.

There is no ghost in that Crystal City cemetery. That is no haunting we feel. Only pride. Only respect. Look at the impossibly long distance Tomás Rivera traveled before he came to rest in the town where he was born: From a family who migrated from their native home, yearly, to pick crops from the fertile American plains to the north, the poorest of the working poor, he became the writer we know, a teacher, and a university president. A great American story. A great Texas story. A great Mexican American story. It may take a ride to a cemetery once in a while to remember, a ritual of respect for an important loss to hush that ghost. It may take a song. It may take a painting. A poem. A fiction. Or maybe a book with them all.

• • •

There is so much misunderstanding about who we are here, where we are from. The extreme Republican right sees us as complicit conspirators with undocumented immigrants who take jobs away from Americans, and as part of the subsequent criminal activity, which begins with an "illegal" border crossing to find work (forget acknowledging the desperation and danger of that), then generates criminal children who overuse the American system of education and health care. The same people and their children, coincidentally, who—much less raging rhetoric on this!—are so valuable for a low-wage, poverty-income workforce which also becomes a rich reservoir for military recruitment, the same people who, despite supporting the American flag by wearing an American uniform, can be accused of disloyalty for equally supporting family with a Mexican flag as well—as if *dos patrias* is unique only to the people of the border, as if Americans who are Irish and Italian and Jewish, for example, don't exist. But even the tanned Democratic left seems to have gained little more than phrasebook insight gotten out of dealing with the maid, nanny, or gardener: After President George W. Bush's last State of the Union address, the Democratic Party offered its formal reply through one of its Easterners, but also asked Antonio Villaraigosa, the rising star mayor of Los Angeles, to represent the West. His reply was in Spanish. That the Democratic Party put him in a position to speak Spanish to a national audience perpetuates an irritating misconception that Mexican Americans are still and forever immigrants, that our English language skills, like our relationship to this country, are for most weak and secondary. The truth is that Latino voters are either bilingual, as is the mayor, or are monolingual English speakers, while those who struggle with their *inglés* see him as a son or brother speaking it as well as they aspire to themselves, and are proud, thrilled, because he is an American, because he is a Mexican American.

Texas was the front line of the historic battle that separated Mexico and the Texas Republic, what became the United States, and the attitude which came of that fight was represented by the treatment of its new Mexican American citizens by a special law enforcement agency known as the Rangers (documented most beautifully by Américo Paredes in his classic *With a Pistol in His Hand*). If that violence is the past, the attitudes that remain are patronizing at best. Even in Texas, Mexican Americans are still considered a foreign, ethnic minority, one far away even when its neighborhood might be less than two blocks north or south. If it's poor, as it usually is, what poverty causes is considered innate, a character trait, never socially caused. At its kindest, the culture is portrayed in a homage in a children's museum, or in a folklorico dance show, and the prevailing unconscious images, framed and shelved, are of men in sombreros and serapes walking burros, women patting tortillas or stuffing tamales in color-frilled white housedresses, while the stories of Mexican adventures are of border whorehouses and tequila drunks—not meant as harmful, only charming, and wild.

And so it has been with matters intellectual and artistic in Texas. That is to say, if it's good at all, Mexican American work can be charming but not serious, not important, certainly not as important. When it comes to literature, the situation has been much worse than for visual art or music. Until very recently, at best, there was no book, no writer, of Mexican descent who was worthy of being taught in a university course on American or Texas literature. Outside those academic rooms, the situation in Texas has been epitomized by *Texas Monthly*, the magazine of Texas, whose stories are never about a Mexican American cultural life that is equal to what gets attention in Dallas or Houston or Austin, which doesn't do stories that aren't seen as oh-so-exotic or oh-so-cute, that are definitely not intended for a Mexican American readership. We are, like Mexicans on the other side, part of the colorful border palate in their land, even part of Texas history, just not deeply enmeshed in the ruling or money class.

•••

Yeah, I know, I've been *muy pesado* for a while here in this, right? By heavy I mean . . . like how about *un poco* bit of fun, eh dude *compa* guy chief *vato*? *Ay ay*, I'm tired of me too, you know? It's hard being an all-important editor, let me tell you. I never been that before either, I admit it. And maybe it's been going to my head, or leaking the lightness out my brains, because I been squishing so long my, uh . . . *ya sabes*.

Entonces, let me go forward, let's move on. And you know what, that's exactly what I mean too! Let's move on! I want *Hecho en Tejas* to be a celebration, a literary *pachanga* with cold beer, frijoles, and, for the few non-vegan tejanos who are left, a couple of cow's heads whose smoked meat we fold into a couple of corn tortillas—or hot dogs on white bread buns *si quieres*, whatever! It is why I invited a few of our singers and songwriters to join in on this anthology because they have acordeones and *bajo sextos* and, unlike me, good voices and can probably dance good too. I invited some artists to spray paint on the walls and wink at your hot tía or primo (you know, *that* one). I broke out the photo album so that we could sit there and remember the old days when it wasn't work but fishing, or when it was holy communion or that crazy wedding and don't you wish you still had that *carro, güey?*

Much as I want *Hecho en Tejas* to be a book that lands in as many high schools and colleges as it can—and should!—or touches as many Michaels and Jennifers, Miguels and Raquels as possible, I also want it to reach every-day readers of all kinds who love Texas. I want it to be a book that so many can learn from, both the young who don't know and the old who do but want it remembered, both those inside the culture and outside. I want it to be a book everyone wants *out*, not in the bookcase, but right there on the coffee table, bumping against the TV. *Look at this!* Go on, put your Coke on it. Drip some chile or Louisiana on page 73 while you're reading. No, that ain't what it's for, but you got napkins and you can use them. That's what they're for. This book is for you to have on your lap.

What I have tried to do is make *Hecho en Tejas* a strong, good read. Not simply as an anthology, a collection of different writers and styles, but as a book with chapters, so that all the voices might form one story, from one family's history. That is, from the front pages to the back, for those who already know a little or a lot about this Texas literature, the book will make them even more proud of the talent, culture, and story, while for those who will find most or all of the material new, yes, they may find a particular poet or writer they especially love, but even without knowing about any single one, what will not be forgotten will be the large of the community as the book puzzles forward, each piece connecting land to history, sorrow to joy, to what is Mexican to what is American, what is assimilated, what cannot be.

I have tried to be comprehensive about our literary history. That it begins with Alvar Núñez Cabeza de Vaca, the Spaniard abandoned on Galveston Island in the early days of the Conquest, the first to live what would become the first mix of Spanish and Indigenous people, should indicate the scope of the volume. *Hecho en Tejas* is hereby a formal announcement: *We have been here; we are still here.* I want this book to overwhelm the ignorance—and I emphasize the *ignore* root of that word as much as its dumb or mean or nasty connotation—about *raza* here in Texas, the people who settled and were settled and still remain in Texas, who will soon be the largest population group in the state, not to mention the region beyond.

TEXAS LIT

Few outside Texas know the writer J. Frank Dobie. He wrote a lot of books, mostly
about Texas lore. My favorites were Rattlesnakes and Apache Gold and Yaqui Silver,
and of course The Longhorns. In Texas he is the Godfather of Texas literature; he
established Texas lit as a literature uniquely its own. I'd highly recommend reading
the father of Mexican American lit, the brilliant Tejano Américo Paredes, his With
His Pistol in His Hand, as important a writer in Texas as Larry McMurtry or
Katherine Anne Porter. This essay too is an intro to an anthology of Texas literature.
A saying in Texas: I wasn't born in Texas, but I got here as fast as I could. Part of my
learning curve.

BEFORE IT BECAME THE feed for the many American stereotypes—and
archetypes—we who live here defend and deflect, what is now Texas was
a territory where many now largely forgotten Indigenous tribes wandered
to and from its coasts and along its rivers and arroyos. Those native people enslaved the Spaniard Alvar Núñez Cabeza de Vaca, an officer on
the shipwrecked Narváez expedition who'd been stranded on a voyage
of exploration and conquest and found himself on the coast of what is
now Galveston Island. His *Relación*, or "Account," of those years is the
first textually recorded tall tale that is set here. Many explorers crossed
from the south what we call the Rio Grande, and this land remained New
Spain until the birth of the country of Mexico, making it the northern

province of Coahuila y Tejas. Then a new force of people came from the east, from places like Kentucky and Tennessee and Arkansas, linking it to the southern United States. In 1836, these new inhabitants declared independence, and so it became the Republic of Texas, the nation of the lone star, for a decade. And so began, with those years, what is the glory and renown of its people and place: From the narratives of the Alamo, to the boom time in ranching and the lore of gunslinging outlaws and sheriffs; from oil wildcatters and rich tycoons, to the modern mediagenic stories of high-rolling business in Dallas and outer space mission control in Houston; unto its famed and infamous politics on the Lyndon Johnson left and the George W. Bush right, the horror of the assassination of JFK in between.

Literatures are often spoken of as encasing a country's cultural identity—think of French, German—or a continent's—African, Latin American. Is Irish literature British? Practically speaking it is, but to some it is no more so than Canadian would be. In the wide and large frame of American literature, publications from and set in the East Coast are tacitly accepted as national, where what lies beyond is called regional—that of the South, Northern California, the Pacific Northwest, the Southwest, and so on, including Texas. Except *this* is Texas. If for no other reason than that it lasted ten years as a country all its own, "region" does not pertain to it. When J. Frank Dobie visited England, he went as a Texan. Larry McMurtry, who does not wear cowboy boots, might live in DC, might write in Hollywood, but there's no doubt about his heritage. Where else could Molly Ivins have gotten her loud humor? The border ballads chronicled by Américo Paredes could only be known alongside our long, legendary river.

Texas has always had these big stories, and the big voices to tell them, too. Several are included in this collection, names familiar across the country, like O. Henry, Barbara Jordan, Katherine Anne Porter, Cormac McCarthy, and Sandra Cisneros. But like much of the United States, Texas is changing its identity—again. If once upon a time it reflected the push away from a history south of the Rio Grande, the Mexican American community will soon represent 50 percent of the population here. Of all places, Texas has been the most ready for this, and of all places, it will become so uniquely. From its longtime adopted love of tacos, enchiladas, and open pit barbeque, to its adobe ranch-style architecture, to its love of color and light, Texas has long embraced its bicultural history. And so it will the new voices that will appear in the newest Texas, the ones who readers of this anthology will become.

Why is it that so many of our own go into a literature class with about as much enthusiasm as most do math or science? Why is it that so many think of those who love literature as being as socially dysfunctional as those who love physics or chemistry?

If I ask a young person to describe a poet or a writer, I commonly get a dreamy description of a very sophisticated man or woman, both with scarves twirled around their neck, keeping warm in a cold climate—probably standing in front of the Hudson or Charles River, or maybe at an Ivy campus, or it could even be Paris or London. And what do they write about? Stories that are intellectual adventures, written beside windows that have views from high above. If important, writers and poets, in other words, live elsewhere, away from the drawls and accents. They do not live here.

Have you ever noticed the joyful, exuberant passion that the Irish have for theirs? Doesn't every one of them know at least one poem by heart? Is it just some kind of native talent? No. It is because they know where they live and love where they live and have pride in who they are and what they do and how they survive. And so it is for us. What more forceful wind than the one that wants to blow down West Texas? What hotter sun than the one that throbs down over the Big Bend? What deeper blue than what carves out the Pecos River? What more powerful light than a lightning storm in the Texas Hill Country? What the Irish understand is that by using their own words from their own land they embolden and nurture their soul. The soul? That oblong whatever-it-is that seems to usually inhabit an area in our body somewhere below our head and above our groin, though sometimes nearer the stomach, or liver, and so on. But your soul does its best artwork when the feet are touching home—when it and you are barefooted, mud squishing between the toes. That's when you're in Mercedes and looking up and seeing that it is *that* sky where the poem has been lurking, or when you're in Lubbock and hearing that wild cousin and knowing that *that* voice is telling the best story. It is when you are *here*, and *here* is Texas.

LA PRÓXIMA PARADA IS NEXT

As in Texas, Mexican American life and culture has been ignored, even seen as belonging to a quaint, unexplainably poor and lesser peoples—naturally suited for non-professional work or, unchecked, crime. What is true is that we are the least educated. That is changing. We are the next stop.

MY GREAT-AUNT, MY MOTHER told me, had traveled from Mexico City to the United States in the 1920s as a world-famous opera star. This sister of my grandmother (she died prematurely in my mother's late teens) had performed in Europe, New York, and finally came to live in Los Angeles, where she was briefly married to a Hollywood director. She became a kind of surrogate mother to my mother, who told me it was through my great-aunt that she'd learned what were the proper, mannered ways of the world. By the time I became conscious of my great-aunt, domestic trouble had overtaken my mother's own life—the only life of hers I knew. I have only a baby's memory reel of my father saying goodbye as he got what were probably his last things. What family she had—her brothers, my uncles—were absent because of money she "borrowed" and who knew what else. My mother was gone too much, dated plenty, and liked to dress plush and drink from cocktail glasses. She was unreliable in action and story. When I was old enough to work, it was for my father, who was the floor superintendent at a downtown industrial laundry—the plant my mother grew up beside. The Anglo boss of at least 200 workers, three-fourths of them mexicanos, my father had grown up in East LA, where he'd learned Spanish. He was a gruff, hard man, an ex-Marine who worked twelve hours a day, six days a week, who would keep this job for forty-nine years, starting as a thirteen-year-old. I learned my great-aunt had occasionally worked for him, too, as a seamstress. She sewed the elastic on bra straps, he told me. I wanted to know if he knew about her fame before. I never asked him much, and he offered few words. She was, he said with finality, just a Mexican.

My father's outlook was undoubtedly tinged with bitterness about being dumped, a divorce. His job did demand him to be *above*, superior, to people who worked for him. If it were only him, it would be only something for me. But I verified the truth of my great-aunt's history years later—the basis of a short story I wrote, "The Magic of Blood," which became a book title of a collection—and what I did was what I have learned we all do with the Mexican in us: We want to overpower the dismissive *less than* given as our being.

It is a structure that remains—yes, of course it's classic sociology of the poor and the rich. But there is more here. For me it's become like a knotted math equation that is essential for a PhD in physics: We are continuously perceived through some not-actual space, not-now time warp, even as the Mexican culture has played so essentially in the history of the American West, so dramatically in the story of this country.

Dramatically? We all know about the Academy Awards. We visualize easily the beautiful golden statue—it's much better known than the logo for the National Basketball Association, though most of us who watch pro games are aware that it is the silhouette of West Virginia's NBA star, Jerry West. Yet does anyone realize that the Oscar is the body of Mexican cinema's legendary director Emilio "El Indio" Fernández, who posed nude for it? This is but a metaphor for what is writ large across the historical landscape that is California and the Southwest and Texas—the names of the mountains, canyons, and rivers, the architectural style that has been most desirable in the past as it is now, and that even became its mass-produced stuccoed-version tract house in the West. The vaquero became a cowboy. Bold colors are everywhere, even among Arizona Republicans. The salsa, tacos, and burritos that have become as unethnically American as pizza, hot dogs, and hamburgers—or almost, because those first three are, still, usually made by Mexicans, cooks who don't count: They aren't really *here*, not their homes, not their families. It's as though American culture is suffering from an ophthalmological disease, call it macular degeneration, and the eyes can't see the faces they stare at, only what is around the field of vision. Or micropsia, which causes objects—Mexican American culture, its people—to be smaller or more distant than they really are. As in a world of hallucinations, we are seen in the distortion of reality that is the visual disease of another who is rich and . . . has a lot more money than us.

Here's yet another way to describe a phenomenon of an unseen yet golden *indio* Oscar: When Americans think of the South, some might think of its White society, antebellum and post, its White literature, its wealth, yet the Black culture is undeniably ever there, present. Others might discuss the history of the South in terms of Black people, their history of slavery, their struggle with poverty, as the homeland of African Americans. This binary is a permanent overlay on the topography of the Southeast region, that quadrant of the United States. It is a Black-White that has come to define much of America's internal history. Now consider a comparable Southwest quadrant, one whose historical binary could be called—should be called—Brown and White. We are all taught passionately about the American expansion into the West, cattle drives, cowboys and Indians, John Wayne movies, but if someone were to say it is the homeland of Mexican Americans, would anyone associate that with populations in Los Angeles, the state of New Mexico, El Paso, San Antonio, the Río Grande Valley? Visitors thrill at oversized enchilada plates and the bountiful bowls of tortilla chips (Americanisms, both), visits to seventeenth- and early eighteenth-century missions, and they see and hear the vast numbers of "Mexican" people who speak to them in homegrown English at shops, stores, and stations—and yet somehow, relaxing in adobe-themed motels or new Spanish villa homes, the binary here is not Brown and White but *blank* and White, the dominant Mexican culture as if from a deserted ghost town. Meanwhile, what Brown people they encounter—who appear in the media—are recent immigrants, invaders from the border. Part of American history? Curiously, if we were to assert that we are part of Mexico's history—which nobody here or there ever has or does—that would be far more of an outrage than the lament that, unless photographed in folklorico costume, we have no images in our nation's history other than as foreigners.

• • •

Mexican American writers have constantly been explaining, self-identifying, or rebelling against the mainstream warp. Though there have been a handful of writers who preceded *el movimiento* (John Rechy, José Antonio Villarreal), it was in the 1970s that an army of insurgent Chicano poets (Ricardo Sánchez, Alurista, Lalo Delgado, José Montoya) romped the cancha as if from a locker room. It took time for an alternate Chicana world to gestate. As it did, in the 1980s,

Gary Soto's poetry from the San Joaquin Valley and Richard Rodriguez's conservative, Castro District nonfiction rose as critically high in mainstream circles as any by Mexican Americans. The childhood-focused New Mexico novel *Bless Me, Ultima* by Rudolfo Anaya sold copies deep into the six figures in its first small-press publication. By the 1990s, women and their stories finally began to be taken up by New York, in particular the work of Sandra Cisneros, Denise Chávez, and Ana Castillo, proclaimed "Las Girlfriends" in no less a mainstream magazine than *Vanity Fair*.

For the last twenty years we have lived on the streets of Mango, an enviable bonanza to Sandra Cisneros, whose activism for reading has made her a star to Mexican Americans everywhere. *The House on Mango Street* has reached every level of the public, from elementary school children who had never touched a book before, to university students getting degrees in literature, but above all to women across the color spectrum. Its success has also mothered a generation of Chicana/o writers preoccupied with the notion that reaching a young adult audience is the key to success. The boom of that literature has had a downside: By virtue of its seeming market appeal, an inference gets made that this represents the intellectual reach of our community. And then there is the Chicana/o world: A direct reaction to the early years of macho, heterosexual *Chicano Power!* (not only male poets, but writers such as Tomás Rivera, Rolando Hinojosa, Oscar Zeta Acosta, as well as Luis Valdez, the acclaimed playwright author of *Zoot Suit*), a successful campaign has seen to it that feminist ideals and goals—through the nonfiction of Gloria Anzaldúa and Ana Castillo, the plays of Cherríe Moraga—are given respect. The use of the slash in *Chicana/o* reflects the doctoral, tenured power of academia and historic reality, demanding that sexual inequality not be reflected even linguistically. The x in Latinx took that further. The downside: The perception by non-gay men and women of too much angry, polemical bashing, that a straight man is treated as a misogynist, a straight woman as a weak victim, and content straight couples are ignored.

For over ten years I taught graduate level creative writing in an MFA program—the direct path of future literature today—and in that time I have seen our young MexAm writers (what I call them—I confess, I *hate* the bureaucratic slash) evolve in complexities. Aware of their community and battles, they are just as concerned with its issues as those from Dostoyevsky, Toni Morrison, Los Bros Hernandez, Sherman Alexie, Terry McMillan. They are from LA and El Paso and Brownsville and Corpus and San Antonio and Albuquerque and McAllen and Laredo and Houston, and though they are familiar with their *antepasados*, these writers do not feel even slightly impaired by it being not that much. Instead, they've come up on Stephen King, S. E. Hinton, Willa Cather, James Baldwin, Poe, J. G. Ballard, Philip K. Dick, Batman comics, Jean Auel, Flannery O'Connor, Alice Walker, Agatha Christie, Jack Kerouac, Terry McMillan. They have learned of writers such as García Márquez and Coetzee. Most of them will openly admit that they do not speak Spanish or very well, that they do not read any Spanish and don't expect to—though they are aware that capital O *others* assume they do. They do not fret over dating outside *raza*, while at the same time claim pride and possession of their own ethnicity and background. The women with men are skilled and ambitious and drink beer and talk about children and marriage—yes and/or no—and movies and contemporary American books they love. The men watch football and basketball on TV and drink beer and eat too many chips while they do— and want to talk about writers like they play on a pro team. The single ones, like single ones from every culture and sexual orientation, are lonely and insecure and, mostly, make bad jokes to compensate. Visiting New York is as desirable as visiting Mexico City. They have all grown up watching, not telenovelas or Cristina, but Oprah and HBO. They have family members who descend from Chihuahua, Guadalajara, Tamaulipas, or who go back generations in El Paso and Corpus Christi. Enraged and saddened by the rejection of the Dream Act, they are not writing stories of immigrants— or cholos, spiritually advanced *indigenas*, border crossings. Instead, their characters—trombone players, convenience store clerks, boring husbands, skinny sisters, cross-dressers—live, like they do, *inside* and part of American culture, not on the outside. They simply believe that if their writing is strong, if they produce enough, New York publishers will want it.

· · ·

In the fall I did a reading in Chicago. I was put up at a gucci hotel downtown, off Michigan Avenue. It is a highbrow shopping area, and when I had some time to take a walk, I crossed paths with David Axelrod, President Obama's well-known adviser. Locked onto on his cellphone, it didn't seem many— the sidewalk traffic was heavy—even recognized him. Directly in front of me were a nicely dressed pair who captured my attention because they didn't seem like anyone else on the street, maybe because they dressed like five-foot twins in matching black sweaters, matching black pants, though I couldn't verify if the black shoes were the same. Newer clothes in an old world, or very hip black? One was wide, the other not. The thinner one carried a shopping bag from Crate and Barrel, which was right behind us at as we waited at a crosswalk, going to the other side of Michigan. Was it the equally long, glossy black hair? Was it that they were both so small? Were they South Asian, Japanese, Filipina? I couldn't see their faces. We were walking past Elan Furs and an Apple Store and approaching Nordstrom. Without being obnoxious (or them knowing I was), I kept pace and stayed as close as I could behind them so I could overhear: One spoke Mexican Spanish, the other, every time, would reply in perfect American English. Neither mixed languages. When they finally slowed at a store window, I saw that the wider one was much older than I would have guessed, while the other was a young woman, maybe twenty. Not once did the older not go all Spanish, the younger all English, as if there were seamless translating buds in their ears.

Our next generation is now here and, though it will listen to the old with respect and good manners, it is fluent in the language of America's busiest literary boulevards.

HUIZACHE

That next big stop in the literature of the Southwest, West, and even in this nation begins with Huizache, the magazine I created for that purpose. Of course, I say that with zero bias! Above, I said that I love Texas. Well, okay, let me rephrase: I love the new Texas that is growing. Not so much the ignorant, despotic, racist old Texas. Let me add here, I am still in litigation—now year seven—with the University of Houston as I work on this book's publication. I will not resign or retire as they wish or claim as "cause," and I will not accept their insulting demand that I teach as the equivalent of a beginning lecturer in English who has just begun a first full-time appointment.

I CAME UP FIGHTING and surviving. I came up expecting to be good at what I did and wanting to catch up, get better, to be better. To not talk it but do it. Where I was, wasn't where I wanted to stay.

I started working at thirteen because I needed money to take care of myself. Making my own money was my own power, my own independence. I worked through high school and through undergrad and grad years where I fed my starving brain. Soon a husband and father, I worked in construction for sixteen years, mostly as a high-rise union carpenter. I wrote stories when I could. When I published a book of fiction that won national literary prizes, change dropped on me suddenly. Though the only courses in English I'd ever taken were the required freshman ones at junior colleges, I became a professor in a well-established and high-quality MFA program. As a student, with no family money support, working, I'd focused on surviving and catching up with other students who always seemed to have gotten their skills and knowledge genetically at birth. Now a professor of graduate writing students, I saw how few like me there were. With my new job, I decided I would let a couple of Chicano students, dreaming of becoming writers, in my MFA workshops as auditors. That got me yelled at loudly, the recognizable roar that preceded getting fired at any construction site. I relented by starting what we called the "illegal, undocumented workshop" that met weekly at my Austin apartment, outside the university's vigilance. Three of those went on to publish notable books. In time, a wider range of Brown graduate students began applying. But with system, history, dominant culture milieu and money and mores, I decided to go another route.

My writing career was doing fine (e.g., multiple times in *The New Yorker*). My life template had changed, though. It wasn't just my own battles and survival anymore. *I* became *we*. Do what for others what was never done for me, for you, for us. Build ladders, throw ropes down, and we climb over walls.

I considered moving on to big-name universities. Good for me probably, as a play in the academic vita game for writers, but they were even less my world, not much better than what I already had as a job. And probably fewer students from the neighborhoods I knew. Then I interviewed at the University of Houston, Victoria, a school not on anyone's map—a tiny college with oil-endowed literary ambitions at the time, in a region that was first an outpost in New Spain, and then Old Mexico, until it became Texas. South Texas, where UHV was, is what I would still call Chicanolandia. The small undergraduate student body was close to 70 percent Mexican American, 25 percent Black. At my interview, when the then president asked me if there had ever been an HBCU type of college campus for Mexican Americans, I decided to push my chips all in.

I believed in a new Texas. Not a kind of progressive's paradise of no guns or less football (naïvely hopeful, my eyes ain't that glazy), but one that had become culturally aware and maybe grateful for the Mexican influence on what has become the American Southwest's allure. Of what made Texas not *de donde vienen los vaqueros*, but cowboy country. I'm old enough to remember the India worship of the hippie era, the Beatles and the Maharishi, incense and Nehru shirts. There was a similar era passing through then, in the love of the musician brothers Flaco and Santiago Jiménez, or Lila Downs. In much of the new Texas, in SanAnto and Htown but especially in tourist-focused Austin, taking off was a new breed of merchant love for all that was Mexican. Its *tacos de todos tipos* and *moles* from black to yellow was not just the food but the cuisine. Spanish colonial was a design style and theme. Huipiles were better than peasant blouses. Frida Kahlo was embraced everywhere as a goddess icon and motif. Bold color was no longer cheap barrio paint, it exclaimed a joy and beauty which openly crossed the frontera.

Huizache was conceived in Victoria, Tejas, and was born in 2011. It was the offspring of the job I was offered and accepted, to teach a class and create and then direct a center for Mexican American literature and culture we called CentroVictoria. Though I had had success in the literary biz—or what's considered success, little income from it aside—mine was as surprising to the industry as it was to me. I knew it was rare, strangely so considering the demographic size of the MexAm community. One major reason was that there were no mainstream venues, magazines, or book publishers that were owned, run by, or financed by a Mexican American—not even editors. We are a poor people. We do exist, but our stories do not exist, unless it is through a category of "us" that represents *us* in *their* eyes and experience, through *their* writers. *Huizache* magazine's goal and purpose was to stand tall on a national stage and *be* our voices and our culture and our own art and our history by our talent and storytellers. Through our own editors who know us, our families, because they are us. No costumed bravado for attention, no it's-all-in-me bragging, no whining and complaining to or shouting at *them* for this and that, just doing it, being it, being us for us. But of course *Huizache*'s for them too, for our own country to see and know our history, our culture here in our own country where we are so little known or seen.

Huizache is a magazine centered in us. Not a magazine that, to seem diverse and open, makes sure to have one Asian, one Black, one Brown in its table of contents. It was and is meant for the dominant literary world to learn about all of us as we are, to stomp down their stereotypes, clichés, and tropes about us, to imagine us in the larger American market. It is and was also for our writers—dismissed and ignored elsewhere—to learn what a professional magazine publication is and does when it is run looking for our best work and the craft and talent it expects, seeing the quality that gets bound in each issue.

And *Huizache* has succeeded. It has received attention in the *Los Angeles Times, San Francisco Chronicle, San Antonio Express-News, El Paso Times, Houston Chronicle, Dallas Morning News, The New Yorker,* and NBC News. And its spectacular list of contributors is easily seen by our readers, but the national recognition they carry with them is often overlooked. Winner and finalist in, awards and fellowships from: MacArthur Foundation, Guggenheim Foundation, National Endowment for the Arts, National Book Award, PEN Faulkner, National Book Critics Circle, PEN/ Hemingway, United States Poet Laureate, Whiting Foundation, Lannan Foundation, Pushcart Prize Stories, Best American Poetry, Best American Short Stories, Best American Poetry, O. Henry Prize Stories.

• • •

The country was Obama's when I took this job. While I was feeling the cooling breezes of a new Texas, I was ignoring that old heat, that I still lived in red hot Texas. Thus I was unprepared for the Trump presidency fall of 2017 when I received an email saying that UHV wanted to end my presence, and thereby what I wrought, on their campus. Unique because I was a tenured full professor, I was not alone. They got rid of all the aged arty "dreck" they had hired with year-to-year contracts (ones with major New York books and anthologies), and they ran off the expensive avant-garde publishing house Dalkey Archive Press and its creator, both of which had been given a treasure chest of promises to move from a lifetime in Illinois to this unknown corner of Texas. Down with those art-set ideas and ambitions, with pride—and responsibility—in getting status as a Hispanic Serving Institution, an HSI. When UHV received that status, and the income attached, the president (replaced) had a huge version of *Huizache*'s first cover in the meeting room of his large office, its art by the great César A. Martínez. That was gone, too.

Anti-art is like anti-mask in a pandemic. Education is believed to be a pro-business enterprise, good for good jobs in oil and shale.

Of course legal engagement commenced between them and me. They believed that I was being uppity, that my or any contract doesn't apply to them (a shockingly hidden fact unknown when doing academic business with the state of Texas). That I should either retire submissively, or accept work that would, anywhere else, be like a hazing for a beginning-est lecturer in English (which is not what my academic degrees are in), the lowest last-minute adjunct hire with all its low baggage. It is true that it did not include janitorial duties, so maybe I do protest too much. (I was a graveyard shift janitor my senior year of high school. The hours were sometimes hard, but I liked the work, and at seventeen I really liked the money.) But my credentials are honored greatly on the vast majority of university campuses across this country, even within the UH system, where at their main campus they have an entire creative writing program of faculty with vitas like mine, just none Chicano or Chicana, Latino or Latina, Latinx.

Their disrespectful thinking became clearer when it came to *Huizache*. In their "or else" demands, my work in CentroVictoria, which was the magazine, went ignored. There was no mention of it. As if *Huizache* just happened somewhere, somehow, and they got Hispanic credit. During our litigation, I asked several times if they would commit to funding it at the beginning of September until the end of August so I could do the magazine's work without having to tell contributors or artists or production people yes, but . . . the issue might not happen . . . and I didn't want to go into the because. The university refused to answer. The only responsible action I could take was to put *Huizache* on hiatus status. That hiatus began in 2019, after our eighth issue appeared.

In 2022 the university cut CentroVictoria. Which ended *Huizache*.

The dismissal is evidence of the value they placed on it and what it represents and does for their university's vision of itself. That is, what our community is and means to them. It was a Trumpian move. They did to *Huizache* exactly what they want and have wanted to do with me and what they think of me and the effing caballo I rode in on.

Is it surprising that Texas didn't respect such a premiere MexAm mag? With its wonderful history of treating us so lovingly along the long border and inside all its cities, legal and penal system, and government bodies? Honestly, sadly, embarrassingly, naïvely for certain, it was to me. I really believed the old Texas and its bigoted disregard for our historical value was over. I really believed in a new Texas, that a new history was being made.

But my creation *Huizache* was not going to be done just because Texas wanted to garbage it. There were other states and regions and cities, especially unbeknownst to certain universities in Texas, where Chicanos have a well-established history. That began with the United Farm Workers in the early '60s with César Chávez and Dolores Huerta. The union originated in the Central Valley of California. The Chicano movement could be said to have begun simultaneously, but Chicano literature's official start was more 1970, on the publication of "El Louie" by José Montoya, who was also in and from the Central Valley of Califas. His brother, Malaquías Montoya, was a seminal and early leader of the Chicano Art Movement. The Central Valley, in other words, is the Chicano homeland. Where else should *Huizache* go to be embraced with joy and respect? To whom else but to the fine fiction writer Maceo Montoya and the university where he is a tenured full professor, the University of California, Davis? Maceo is heir to a family tree that is as rooted to a land as a huizache tree, and he is now heir to a magazine that is grateful for that lineage and history. Proud as I am of what *Huizache* has done thus far, I am as proud to pass it forward to this man's lead, as excited to see what comes, relieved that it has such an ideal new home.

Ladders are standing, tied ropes hang down—climb!

SNOW ANGEL

Story of a few days in winter, February 2021, when this disabled man—that'd be me—didn't believe he'd survive days of 20 degree and less temperature predicted, alone, without power or heat, snow-trapped in his Texas home.

EVERYBODY WHO WATCHED ANY local TV news—like local newspaper reading, it's possible that too may be in major decline—knew a week before that a continental mass of Arctic freeze was drooling southward onto central Texas. It was going to be real winter cold in Austin, where it's mostly real hot seven to nine months a year.

I was normal, maybe even better than average aware. You warm wrap your outdoor water spigots and let them drip. You set aside some drinking water. You cover your sensitive outdoor plants. I had a down bag, I think 15 degree (or -15, not sure), but it was warm. I'd had a good load of groceries delivered a couple of days before. They said up to a few inches of snow, weren't sure it wouldn't be the number one, two, or three coldest weather recorded in Austin since once in the late '40s or once before the turn of the last century.

But I started getting worried all day that Sunday before. It was like the hours before a cold or worse is coming on, a general unease, misgiving, dread. My ex in El Paso—still my closest friend—didn't understand what I could be worried about. I had food, water, warmth. So what if I couldn't drive out a day or two. I agreed but still worried inexplicably. I wanted to go to sleep but, tired, even had done plenty of Fitbit minutes, I wasn't relaxed enough for bedtime. When I finally forced myself under the covers—my down bag actually—I shifted from one side of my body to the other. It was the tree, I decided. I have a large white oak in my backyard that leans toward my bedroom and, incidentally, toward me. Its lean is a degree or two on an angled line to smack the roof above and then the pillows at the head of my bed. Of course, it wouldn't fall all the way down if it went, but it bothered me so much—the expense of fixing the roof alone—that years ago I had called a tree man to maybe cut it down, beautifully full grown though it was. He assured me it was safe, but he did cut off a few heavy limbs on the leaning side. That Sunday night in my bed, I visualized . . . what if this record cold storm, with the record snow, the heavy ice, what if the fates, the who knows what. . . . I moved myself and bedding needs to the comfortable living room couch. That was a lot better. It was snowing, I could tell by the quiet. I fell asleep probably around 3:00 a.m.

• • •

I woke up before 7:00 a.m. It was cold outside my bag. I think my weather app said eight degrees outside the house. I also noticed that the phone was only 79 percent charged. I checked a light switch. No light. No power. It wasn't the first time this had ever happened here. I'd lost power more than a few times, once because the box on a pole a street east of mine exploded, but only for a few hours. I'd gotten an email from Austin Energy telling all to reduce power use from Sunday to Tuesday to help the system out. There was a phone number to call if the power went out. I called that and it rang only a couple of times before a nice lady answered.

She very kindly said it probably was the rolling blackouts. They were happening across the state.

The state? I asked if she was sure and couldn't she know for sure? I was thinking about that electrical box on the pole over there. No, she wasn't sure. But probably it'd be back on in a few hours. Though it might take a day given the snow.

A few hours, or it might be a day?

It could be a day or even a few days, she said. No longer than Friday.

Right then I believed it would be at least until Friday. I always prefer expecting the worst case and planning on it.

She was very sweet-sounding. She didn't say a cheery good morning, but she could have. She wasn't trying to hide anything she knew or thought. She was always this way, unworried and kind. Perfect for this phone job because she didn't think about what she was saying in a long, consequential sense.

Or at least she hadn't yet. Mine was an early call. It was answered so fast, like there were many service folks like her—I doubt it—or there had been few calls like mine yet. More likely. Maybe she'd just signed in. Probably working remotely from the comfort of her home even, due to the pandemic, with her power and heating on.

My battery was down 10 percent more after that call. I did have a battery charger. It could do two full charges. But I use my phone too much maybe, and it is an old one and its battery is weak, and normally I have to charge it three times during the day if it's not connected. Two full charges isn't that many hours of use.

I calculate what it is. Unless I get lucky, very probable I will be here alone. I say up to Friday, and maybe worse. I have food. I have some water and I can and will get more before it totally freezes, if that's what happens—I don't know. I have food. I am making myself warm. But I am alone. If I were with someone, I could do this, we could, I'm sure of that. Alone, I feel very uncertain of myself and my abilities.

I go ahead and text a few friends. It's not too early for urgency, but they sleep with Do Not Disturb on their phone like most of us. I get one text back fast from a friend who lives behind me. He has no power.

I send out a few more texts and leave a couple of voice messages. I do searches for info.

The smart answer is: Don't stay in your house for three or four frozen nights alone. My phone is 20 percent less battery now. I call El Paso and ask my ex to please book me the closest hotel for today. I give her the name of the closest one, tell her to reserve and pay it, but if there are no rooms, whatever hotel downtown. Don't think money.

Another friend texts that they have power. We talk on the phone. She insists I come stay with them.

Get a Lyft, she says. It makes me feel good, relieved. I'm still half thinking I should wait. Maybe the power will come back on. We decide to talk again in an hour or so, to save battery. It's in the 50 percent range now.

I check UberLyft apps. No available cars. Easy to predict since there's probably no driving whatever in this city so unprepared for snow.

I pull out my winter clothes. I even take out long underwear but not to wear yet. A Patagonia pullover, an East Coast neck scarf, a long overcoat, thick gloves. I have a good wool watchman cap or two somewhere. I open my front door and my neighborhood looks like Wyoming or Denver. They will say it was a record six inches, nothing really in a heavy winter culture, but that's a lot to me. There are snowy houses across the street with no driveways and no lawns or any street or curbs. There are no moving cars. Just snow and silence.

Without much clarity, I begin to organize the brain for the cold. I cannot walk to a neighbor's house because I don't walk that steadily when there *isn't* snow. More confessionally: I'm afraid of this snow because I know I am likely to fall hard. I had a brain injury over a decade ago. I lost a lot of the use of my right side. My arm and hand and fingers, my leg too stiff. Once athletic, I can't run ever again. I walk poorly but stubbornly without an aid, often enough pretty good considering. Sometimes not. I am not stable. I lived in Laramie for four snowy months in way-back times, 1994. The most snow I'd ever seen. Once I fell like in a cartoon, like I was trying to do a backflip and only made it up to horizontal when plop, straight down on my back. I popped right up, worried about my laptop, not my body. That flop would not be well received by this body now, and it won't pop up in my best moments.

A text from El Paso. I have a room at the hotel a few miles away. The temperature outdoors is fixed at 12. I think the coldest weather I've ever walked in is 15 with a harsh wind in New York City.

I do not like the feeling of being fragile. Of being old and scared. Of being disabled. I am a functionally well-off disabled, I always tell myself. I try not to complain. So many much worse.

A good friend around the corner texts that they are powerless and heatless. She has on many, many layers. She thinks it's smart to get out, but she can't because her husband is in quarantine. His elderly mother was in a senior home whose power went out days ago, who knows why, and he had to help her move to a hotel, and she has COVID. Now my friend and her husband are together in separate rooms. He can't go anywhere, so she can't either.

Another hour has passed, no power rolling in anywhere, and I call my friend in north Austin who said they'd come. Tells me to get a bag together, that they're on their way. Some time passes, then she texts that their truck barely made it beyond their driveway. She and her husband and a neighbor are trying to get it out of the rut. A half hour later, maybe more, she asks if I can get there by Uber or Lyft. Or a taxi. Maybe hire a tow truck except I'd be the tow.

I call the 311 info line. It's a wait and a lot of battery use but I finally get through. I ask if there is any specific information about the power outage. What neighborhoods, and how long?

No sir, the woman says. She's a little more businesslike than her counterpart earlier, just sharp, direct. She's had, I'm sure, more than a few calls this morning.

Do you know what the city is expecting and suggesting to those of us who don't have power or heat?

She tells me they're hoping it will all come back on soon in the affected areas, but they don't know exactly. Best is if you just keep as warm as you can. If you feel like you can't, we have a "warm center" downtown.

But there's no way to get downtown.

It's like she hadn't considered that.

She suggests a taxi.

Thinking Uber or Lyft, I say I tried that. I think, fire can't come, police can't either.

She suggests I stay with family.

My family is in El Paso, a son now in Tampa. I'm alone.

She suggests friends.

They're stuck. We're all stuck where we are.

She doesn't have more because there is no more.

31 percent battery, 12 degrees outside according to the app, still 44 inside if the thermostat is right. There are no cars available for Uber or Lyft.

I text a former neighbor who used to live next door but had to move in January. He'd cared for the elderly couple, friends, who lived there for maybe forty years until they passed a year ago. The house is empty now, needing repair. He says of course he can come. They are staying in an apartment nearby, no power or heat either, but they have a propane cooker and he will even grill us all some carne for dinner. *Muy mexicano*, he tells me *of course* I can stay with them. He has his truck and can come get me. This sounds okay but I tell him we should wait until like 2:00 p.m. (it's almost 1:00) because there's that part of me that can't believe they wouldn't get the power back on by then. Also, it will be as warm then as it's going to get. He says okay, to call him back.

As careful as I've been, I now have 14 percent battery. I try my battery charger. Instead of four blue dots, there are only two. Suddenly I'm more panicked. But through the kitchen window, I see my neighbors across the street. Their little children—I've watched them grow from bumps in their mother's belly to screaming toddlers from my side of the window—are excited about the snow. I open the front door. Snow almost to my welcome mat. I have finished saltillo tiles on the front porch, and I dare not step there because it will be like stepping on oiled glass.

I yell, Are you guys doing okay? Warm?

He yells back they'll be fine. They have a fireplace. Asks about me.

No fireplace, I say. Latest worry is this phone dying.

I want to say more but he's running inside his house. Running. He can run. Then he's back out shuffling through the powder—making sure each foot is on the ground the whole time—across the street to the edge of my front porch.

He has a few of these solar chargers, he says, handing me a gadget the size of a thick smartphone.

It's easy to hook up. And just call me if you need more.

Let's exchange numbers, I say. I won't try to explain why we never had before because there is no explanation.

When he handed me his charger, it was with that pandemic distance we all know well, his arm reaching out like only his fingertips could cross the imaginary limit, a cautious lean in. We all have different interpretations of the six-feet requirement, its courtesy and/or fear. But his was not that. He tells me that he's being careful because he had a fever the night before and thinks it's COVID. (Later, it will be confirmed.)

I can't think of more to say than how very sorry I am, that I hope it's a light case. I say to let me know, call me.

I plug the charger into my phone. Four blue dots. I message him a huge thank you. I hear my brain saying *go*. I call my former next-door neighbor. Can you come? Now? Yes, he's on his way. I am feeling like the chance to get out, the possibilities, are closing. That I have only a few hours left and then I'm here, like this, for days. He calls after about fifteen minutes and says he's having trouble but he will keep trying. I tell him to try but don't do anything dangerous. *He* thanks *me*. Thirty minutes later he texts *mi troca nomás patina*, his truck just slides.

I am stuck until Friday. Nobody's coming, nobody can. I do have food and water. I have a down bag and clothes.

311 is busy. I call 911. I tell the woman who answers I don't have an emergency now, but I might and I just want advice. To prepare. She doesn't like my call. Just an easy question, I say. Is there anyone to call in an emergency to come for me if somehow I get into trouble while I'm trapped here?

Disabled, I can't walk out. She can't help me, she says sternly. Call 311, she demands.

I check UberLyft—nothing—so now I am setting up for my stay. I can only find a half-burned votive candle. Though I could have sworn I had two boxes of candles, it's been years. I only remember the cute little holders and I don't find them either, or I dumped them all myself somehow. I find a big old red Christmas candle. I remember its small flame. I have a flashlight but only one, the other with a dead bulb. I check UberLyft, nothing. I go to my car in the attached garage. I start it and dial around the stations, but nobody is talking about the power outage in Austin—much less what is being done about it—and I can't take the happy or sweet or clever commercials. I look for a plug to charge the phone but no. I could stay in here, recline the seats, for a few hours every day. Maybe sleep with the heater on, the engine on, windows cracked. I check UberLyft, nothing. I unlock the garage door and I leave it a quarter open to let air in and out.

I grew up in LA smog. I spent many years in desert El Paso heat. I've never lived in the cold West or East and would never. Chicanos on skis? Are you kidding? I like the beach, but I don't want to hang way out in the ocean to get chewed by sharks. I'm not unadventurous, just aware of my strengths and weaknesses and skills realistically. I've been in serious *broncas* with bad dudes. I've been a biker bar bouncer. Once I did a few days hike in Glacier National Park in Montana with two high school friends who'd become silver miners in northern Idaho. I was strong and brave then, young, howling fearless, or almost. We saw a grizzly bear from a high path on the opposite side of a river, and I decided I was not a mountain man. That bear was so huge I didn't want him or her to ever see me again.

I didn't know how I would do in this freeze, all by myself, alone. With my disability, my inabilities, easy things are hard. The seemingly easiest things can be the hardest. Signing my name, gone. Cutting food, cooking. Typing. I am slower with only one working hand. I make a ton of typos, but all I have to do is be patient. Right? I try, sincerely, but I am hyper, hot-blooded, more *go go* than *wait, calmly, wait.* I hold my phone with one hand. All I have is one hand, with a little help with the troubled right. I could go on. Add stress. Add lack of sleep. In this cold, I am scared of me and what can be my errors and misfunctions. With someone else around, it might not be a fun time, but we'd make it, and I'd be a help. If three to four days in twenty degrees high and single digit lower, I give myself, coldly, all alone, 50-50.

I check UberLyft. Nothing.

In utter silence, all by myself, alone. I want to love silence. I do. I want to be a Zen master and purr in the silence. The silence I do love is in a rage of birds, a river, wind, frogs, crickets, cicadas, gulls, waves. The silence here is no cars or trucks, no highway, no copters, no jets, no TV over there, no ranchera music blasting farther away, no nada. The reflection of the so-white snow is the only loud. It is and will be me and me and whatever the brain is streaming. Honestly, I'm not Zen enough.

I keep checking UberLyft every 10, 15 minutes. Nothing.

I'm officially organizing. Where I will sleep. And sit most of the next days, the couch. Doors I close. In the kitchen I momentarily panic because I can't find matches. I open every drawer and cupboard until I remember a basket where I'd scooped a thousand little nothings, and yes, there's a wrapped set of Caballo Rojo matchboxes from Spain or Mexico for smoking Cuban cigars. I don't know where to start to light the oven in this stove. The burners are easy. Or should be. I can't figure out how to light a match with one hand. It pains my unsteady soul that *this* is hard for me, too. When I finally spark one, I almost burn myself. I finally figure out to hold the box with the bad right hand and strike with the left. I light the burners.

No Ubers, no Lyfts, no little digital bug cars anywhere, nothing.

I have to surrender. I don't feel like leaving the gas burners on is fire smart, or good for breathing, but for emergency warmth, they're it. And the car. I'm not happy but what choice do I have? There is lots worse. The shellings in Syria. The floods in Honduras. There are those who cross the Sonora desert alone, in 100-plus degrees. There is dying of COVID, no breath.

I have to save my phone's power. I can't let myself hope there will be another charged charger if. But I do have, by my calculations, an hour. At 4 it will be the "high" temp of the day, and then, like the sun, it will drop lower on the horizon and be dark in the house and then another storm and then colder.

When I check Uber, are those real options for a ride from my home to the hotel? Really? Comfort, UberX, UberXL. I take seconds to not pick wrong, but I have to be fast and, still guessing, choose Comfort because it'll be a better car. Screen changes. Yes to this, yes to that, and *pop*, I have a digital bug car coming! The driver's a few miles away, a familiar area near the river. He will have to cross a bridge. Austin bridges always ice in below-freezing temperatures. He was 12 minutes away. He is 12 minutes away for an uncomfortably long time, not moving. I don't know how long I am staring at the screen. A long, long patient time. Maybe he's dropping someone off. Maybe he's stuck. Probably stuck. I text him. *Do you think you can come for me? Are you able to come?* There is no reply. *Are you there?* That one takes a long time in the Sending status until a red sentence appears that there is a connection problem. Of course, I don't believe he can come, nobody can. He has no phone to contact him, I don't know why. I text, *I understand if you can't make it, but can you call me please and let me know?* I just want to know if this is real, if this can happen. I've searched the screen and there are no other car bugs anywhere. I don't want to cancel him, but what if things have improved and there are a few drivers now and I will miss them waiting? Which I know is unlikely but. My last text doesn't get through and I resend. It will not go through. I resend again and wait on the pinwheel. And then, like a reboot, it says he is five minutes away.

I watch his bug car's staccato jumps along nearby streets like it's an action movie. Five, four, three minutes away. Every stop and turn. Every pause a possible End. He goes, he goes. Instead of turning south onto the access road along I-35, where he would run into my street and turn east, go under the highway and onward, he continues straight, past the line of my house, where he will turn south and then west, in other words circling to my house. GPS must have sent him that way. And then he is on a street on the higher side of mine and is approaching construction barriers right at my street. The city put them up a week before because of a broken water line. Cars are warned of the dead end a block before mine, and if he were to detour into the steep, jagged streets behind my house, he and his car would spend a week stuck in the frozen snow.

He doesn't. He stops. He texts: *I'm sliding on ice. I'm stuck.* It's a steep hill there, too. Time passes. *OK, I got out but now I can't go farther.* Then, *I can't go any farther.* I say, *The construction, I know, you are so close*, but really, though I'm trying hard, I can't think what or how next. He writes, *Can you walk here?* I can walk there with no snow, but I will fall with it. I'm not sure I won't fall ten feet from my front door if I make one step out. No, he can't walk to me, he won't. *I can't*, I write, *I am disabled.* I say, *I'll give you an extra $50.* I should have offered more but I don't want to sound like a nut job, do I? *Ha!* he writes back. He says, *I'm sorry, I can't get there.* His bug car is turning around. He hasn't clicked me off. *Listen*, I write, *if you are going back the way you came, one more try?* I tell him about the access road along the highway and a left turn straight up to my house. *OK*, he texts back.

And the bug car turns onto the digital access road, makes a left onto my digital street and then under the highway. That bug is digitally squirming going up—it is uphill, meaning thick snow—onto my street. I go to my front door to see if, unbelievably, the real car could—when there he is, at the top of my driveway! I am ecstatic, half numb from the blow of reality. I text: *I'll get my bag, be right out, can you pull into the driveway?* That's so I walk the least, reduce the slip and fall chances.

Which, bad suggestion, big mistake, he does. My driveway tilts downward.

I am reluctant to step onto my saltillo tile porch. I shout if he could come and help me. He steps out of his car and stands and stares at me. I tell him that I'm sorry but that I think I need help walking.

He doesn't reply but, after a pause, he walks carefully in the snow to me. I give him my bag.

If I can just put my left hand on your shoulder, I tell him, that usually helps me walk steadier.

He stares at me and his hands are at his face, moving.

You're deaf, I tell him. You can't hear me.

But he knows the help I'm suggesting without words. He swings the bag over his shoulder—he's a big young guy, a gimme cap covering his forehead, late twenties to early thirties, six one or two, over 200 pounds—and we step together. Of course, I slide the second step I take, but since I have my hand on his shoulder, I can handle it. The next step or two it's his foot sliding, but easy adjustment, and we are on a concrete walkway, and we are at the car doors, and he opens mine and lets me get in, and he gets into the driver's side, and the Uber car starts. I am getting out! I am not 50-50 to survive the igloo freeze by myself, in a stupid power outage cold, probably no phone, scared of myself alone and my damaged abilities, days silently waiting hoping alone.

He was the only available Uber in Austin. The only and the last—the last for several days to follow—and he came for me. Why, how? UberLyft drivers drive because they need to make money to live, because they don't have enough money. Probably he didn't realize that there were no other Ubers out, didn't realize that conditions were as bad as they were. He didn't know he was really an angel sent by God to save me.

The car starts scooting sideways, wheels spinning, as he backs up on my inclined driveway, then slides back down. This goes on until we are diagonal. I talk, suggest, but he's deaf, he doesn't hear me, his backseat driver. We have to communicate. There are no other humans to translate our cultures and words. We become primitive men on primordial earth, neither of us a common language. I make my hand signs, motions, to tell him to back the car onto the lawn, don't worry, and turn around that way. Yes yes, more more, all that he doesn't hear from me as he gets the car pointing the other way. Then he whales on the gas and the back tires spin. We both get out of the car, and he digs snow with his hands ahead of the front tires. I am not positive, but I think it's the back tires that need help, some sticks of wood for them to jump on and over, but we both agree in making shoveling motions with our hand language.

I step very carefully to my garage and go in for the small flat shovel I have. He scrapes all he can in front of the car to the street. I feel worthless, prematurely ninety-nine years old, I can do so little to help him. I am torn between walking, and maybe falling, to be near him and where the action is, or just sitting, no potential injuries, pathetically in the back seat, not adding more trouble. It takes some time. Fifteen minutes at least, could be more. I will tip him well, I promise. All I can do for him is give him money. I cannot believe, I'm sure he cannot believe this either. When he's ready, I point to his car's trunk several times for him to keep the shovel. It's his now.

He steps on the gas and the car climbs, as jagged as a digital bug, but it retreats. Again and again, he tries, he gets close. He gets out and takes the shovel to move more snow he thinks may be impeding the front tires, never near the back ones, and he stomps on it until we stop, almost facing sideways. I am now imagining we are stuck, he will stay with me, and though it will be a freezing silence for both of us. . . . But he steps on it steadier a few times. I am getting excited, I am yelling *yes, just a little more, don't let up on the gas, don't stop!* He is so close. I yell, *Just jump the curb if that's where it's going, don't try to fit it in the driveway,* but thankfully only God can hear me, not this driver. He doesn't hear me, and he shouldn't. He does not need me . . . when then the right tire hops over the curb and we are on the snowy street and I let out an unmuted howl of *yes yes yeah you did it you did it!*

I put my left hand on his big shoulder from the backseat and slap it a couple times. We drive downhill and it becomes steeper a little way from my house. Two cars have been left there on the uphill side. Our car fishtails some going down, but it can and does stop at the light, where it flattens. The last long leg to the hotel is a downhill too, but, though we encounter no cars in either direction, there are tire ruts to ride in, even if we feel the car sliding a couple of times. And then a right turn, a left, a right, and it's the hotel. I am safe. I am rescued.

He comes around not because I wait for him but because I am slow to swing my legs out the door. He gets my bag and reaches his hand to pull me up. I am also, I think, in a bit of survivor shock that I am here. Up, I get my usual unsteady balance and he sets himself so I can put my left hand on his right shoulder to step to the hotel doors. I don't think I need to, except there is snow, and I do it. When we pass the first set of doors, in the dry area, he backs off. He does not make a bye-bye sign we all know, but raises his hand for goodbye. I say, out loud, *thank you, thank you so much*, and he doesn't hear me, he can't, but that doesn't matter, and I want to, in this COVID world, at least touch my hand to his shoulder, only he is already out the door, looking ahead, hearing far beyond me.

Seems like a good finishing essay to me. Maybe it's all—all the above essays—because I am a man and was once a boy. I don't think so myself—my mom could dropkick most dudes, drink any under the table, and then count her winnings—but if so, I plead guilty. This isn't really about male instincts though.

FIGHTS

This most recent piece, the last here. We live. We make mistakes. I have lived, I've been a fool and made foolish mistakes. This one I write about, and this one I want to apologize for privately, here in public. Not that big as mistakes can go—nobody died, we walked and talked and got old, and yes, I've done worse—but it has haunted me all this time.

I ALREADY KNOW WHAT everyone thinks these days. And these facts undeniable: I am a boy. I grew up a boy and became a man. And yes, I did those dumb boy things and then dumb man things. Very few of those boy ones—my focus here—were supposed to be praiseworthy or particularly smart or even laughable, even while other boys-then-men might laugh. None of it is taken for granted anymore either. Worse, most of what doesn't involve books and learning and being a very good student isn't either. Like playing around using hands and legs as if they were born with boy toys meant for fun, and muscles for more and even better, which maybe led boys to what is called too macho. Or another word for that, a kinder one, like jerk.

Consider me backward and fucked up because all my boyishness grew into my mannishness—whatever I am called. I'm saying this: That it's okay, I'm fine with it, and sorry if it's stupid and some will shake their better-than-me head and roll their better-used eyes because for me types it's a basketball night on TV and I don't feel like going to a reading event, say poetry or fiction, or a body/spirit healthier talk. Which, to make sure you understand, I can like occasionally. If you really won't lighten up, get all Sunday school stern on me, screw you. Now if that's an instance of me being macho, a jerk, and you can't laugh, I accept it. It happens you can thank my mom—she drank and laughed hard—for teaching me her attitude. And for the record, our worlds might not overlap, but I am a lot nicer than she was.

I'll go with this: Boys and girls are different. Is it those small anatomical or biochemical items? Probably. I am no expert on either boys or girls, but I will say certainly that the two behave differently. More certainly said, I know boys do. Do girls as teenagers drive chrome wheels, low or high, or roll old drunk dudes for a whatever it is, a pint or even half-pint, already so *pedo* they almost don't know they been rolled? Do boys, nice to look at but really meaner than chained dobies, blink long black lashes, lavender eye shadow above and slinky blouses below, daring you to not stare, then laugh at you and wink when you *ay ay, mamí*? Both cruise the boulevards, but which, if you stare too long, or "wrong," don't just not smile but throw the eye on you, like you're the one who ran off with their baby girl or their coin or cred or who the fuck you think you are, *puto mamón*?

Though not all act out the same, every boy is aware of a fight being close, getting hit or having to hit, dealing with this junk daily. Like sex, it's something every boy thinks about whether they like to or never have and hope maybe—in the case of fights—won't ever. They know, *know*, they might have to or fear they can't or won't but know, *know*, that going out there, it is always a *there* there. All at a vaguely minimum worry, but a few, whatever the cause or source, can't avoid it. Like me. Not the most, but enough. I was a boy who had a couple of those school fights we remember. One in junior high where all the kids in the yard piled around like it was a wild exciting musical event, following the sound. I don't remember how that ended, running off probably, or if I got suspended or what next. I got suspended for a few things I don't remember. In high school it was me and a football star of the not-that-great football team. That fight went on in the hall before a first period bell, lockers on either side, teachers even watching, until the stupid star tried to tackle me, couldn't, and my upper cuts were low, easy with his head at my stomach, accurate. Actually dangerous. It was stopped quick after a few of those. We both got a week off. I was a boy who, with a buddy, got jumped in an alley close to home. A kid had me down until I hit him in the face with a rock my right hand found. I was a boy who hung with the baddest dude—at least a year too old for his grade. As number two, I got more attention than he did. I was a boy, one day walking in The Dips (a hilly open field), who stabbed a Black kid below the shoulder with a dull switchblade because he was just enough bigger than me and we were staring at each other in that way, like we had to. Both of us shocked, I ran like I could go back in time a day, an hour. I ditched school for a week, waiting for LAPD to drag me off.

These were pre-adult bouts and fears. These were the halcyon days (had to look up that ancient word!) long long ago, before real amped bad boys carried Uzis and automatic weapons.

All that to get to another boy story, related but private, mine. Or is it only mine? That I didn't like me very much then. I didn't know why I had so much unhappiness. I'm not saying I couldn't make a list of shit. And I'm not saying I couldn't backtalk that list and say tough shit baby boy, grow up, get real, there's a ton worse. Even then I thought that. What I wanted was a friend I could trust. You know, a friend, a *compa*, a brother. I found one when I was fourteen. Call him JD. He wasn't from the neighborhood. He was poor. His sister was, his mom too, though she worked nights at a hospital. Somebody else paid their rent, government or church. His dad, I learned way later, was a drunken asshole who rode a Harley. He never gave them two nickels. JD was the skinniest kid I'd ever known. His mom bought his sister and him fruit. Sacks of apples and oranges or pears, bananas like on a tree branch, ones I'd never seen before. Nobody had fruit at home like this. If there were where I lived, I'd have eaten as many as my stomach could bear—grocery bags full!—like they were Eskimo Pies. He said he and his sister were allowed two a day. And that's all they ate, unless I was there. Then he got himself one, me another. He took schoolbooks home to read or study. He listened to radio stations I didn't know how to find. He was way ahead of me on everything—in the same way he was running miles every day, way farther than my imagination could go. I'd never heard of track. I thought running laps was more a punishment, or what boxers did for pain endurance.

And yet JD wanted me to be his friend. I didn't know why exactly. Maybe because he didn't have any other friend. I liked to have a friend like him. I had other friends for other things. I had girlfriends. He didn't. That may have been another reason I was a hero for him. I was bigger than him, he was older than me. But I'm saying it was because I could do, would do, what he wouldn't alone. Like steal a car. Borrow it. We did it a couple of times and just drove around. I should've been driving, but I definitely didn't have a license. Maybe he did. Nah. No matter, he didn't look the type who'd borrow someone else's car without permission, and I was like a hot chick to cops—they noticed me whenever they saw me. They wanted to know everything about me and feel around. Once JD found a car, an ugly Studebaker, that he could start with a butter knife. It belonged to an old couple who never seemed to be awake at dark and didn't seem to need it in daylight either. JD had a place he wanted to go: A club in Hollywood called the Whisky a Go Go to hear the Animals. I'm sure I'd heard of the club because of the dancing girls in cages and pretended to know the band. He drove us there—fun night!—and back at like 3:00 a.m. JD introduced me to a world unknown to me.

JD wasn't the kind to ditch but I did for all kind of reasons. So he got to thinking. JD'd never been to Disneyland and wanted to go. He found a bus, roundtrip, and we could make it back like he'd been to school when he got home. He had strict hours because of his mom and sister. Next time he wanted to see the beach, so we hitchhiked. Hermosa Beach was a straight shot down Artesia Boulevard, only a few strange rides with drawling pervs and drooling who-knew-whats and kind weirdos.

We were on our way home, salt still coating our skin, sand in our pockets and underwear. We were at a busy corner on Artesia when a VW bug caught JD's eye. Two boys, I'd guess eighteen years old, plus or minus one. They were Nazi white, with prick haircuts of the day, almost a fade on the sides and a flat buzz fuzz on the top. They were growling. They both shot me the finger, the driver reaching across the passenger so I could see his erect digit even if he couldn't stick it in the wind out the window like his partner. They were saying fuck you to me to make sure I understood how they felt.

I was fearless to JD. I knew this was a feature that drew him to me. I guess it was my reputation—I didn't ever brag to him—anyone actually—about fights or encounters I had. But for a few months I had a girlfriend who lived across from where he lived. It might have been how I even began knowing him, I don't remember. The girl—she was fourteen, ninth grade, and we didn't last that long. I liked playing with her, but she scared me too much about wanting to have a baby. Though it seemed like years later, as months do when you're that young, it probably wasn't so long after that her new boyfriend sent over the ugliest, scariest dude anybody had ever seen—he had to duck his head under the door header to get into the garage where me and JD were—to pass me a warning: Don't go near her ever again. I just laughed. Because it was funny that Frankenstein was there about tiny her—already forgotten by me—to back her sorry boyfriend. I assured the monster, and he believed me too, because it was way true. When he left, me and JD really laughed. Me because the dude was a cartoon character and she was kinda shaped like one too, JD because I didn't flinch. He thought that was fearless, I think because he didn't consider that it was mostly stupid. It wasn't that long after we heard that the girl dropped out of school, PG.

JD looked at me to get my attention. The Nazis had no interest in JD being there, I knew it, he knew I knew it. I glanced back to them, revving their car's whiny motor. I said fuck you sideways, then looked completely away from them, meaning to dismiss them bye-bye. They peeled ahead and squealed right, motor popping, looped behind us, and both got out. They were both bigger than me, though not by so much by height as by muscle. Don't remember a single word between us, though there were some. Only one Nazi stepped up—pretty sure they decided while standing there, knowing it was only me and not me against both, that being their kind of honorable, and the bulkier one began his beating of me. He was skilled like a trained boxer, every shot on target, hurting. I always felt quick to move and pop, and I hit him, but his were three to my one, and, though it doesn't matter, I can't imagine I hurt him a little. I can't remember a moment I didn't feel on defense. I didn't feel like I was going to go down, but that was because I very fast knew I had no chance. I backed down. Surrendered. I don't remember them leaving. I don't remember me and JD hitching home. I don't remember one conversation we had inside a car, getting out of a car, saying see you later, saying shit or walking, eating, going to bed, waking up. I did see that I had a broken nose. I'd felt that early, before I knew it would get worse.

I don't know how long I was too messed up to talk to anyone. I can't explain why I ached but not so much on the body, only humiliation and shame. I don't remember thinking something like *everybody knows* even. Not sure I'd have cared if that was true, but I don't think I cared any more than when I'd won a fight. I didn't dwell before. Except this time. But only JD knew it happened. I couldn't figure out how to be with him. How to explain. It wasn't like he would tell anyone, shame me more. I even knew he was on my side, that he felt bad for me.

I don't know how long it was before we hung out again. I started favoring other friends. I saw a girlfriend. When I finally did see him, I lied. I tried to act like how I was before. I said, casual like, that I'd gotten in another stupid fight. Two guys again, I said, and this time both. I didn't bring up their age or size because that wasn't the point maybe. No details of the nothing that didn't happen. I told him, like, can you believe that? And of course he couldn't and didn't. Only a fool would have believed me. And he was not stupid, no fool. But he was so smart he knew I wanted him to believe me, so he didn't say he didn't. He didn't say anything, and it never came up again. Like my beating never happened either.

I have never forgotten. It always comes up in my head. I'm still embarrassed by that lie. Not the fight when my ass got kicked big-time. I'm ashamed that I made up that lie. I still don't think I can even tell him this to his face now. But I want to say to him, the man him now, thank you for letting that boy me get by with it.

Boy things doing nothing that mattered. Or should not have mattered, or only mattered too much to me back then. And yet carried on silently. Things changed with us. I think he probably thought less of me as I thought, stupidly, less of me for that lie. We did hang out a few times the next couple of years. I'd moved again with my wayward mom. I saw him moving on, moving up, and still whatever changes were happening, I still wanted to be seen and liked as he saw me and my life before. As if I knew whatever that was before. I felt like he couldn't and shouldn't trust me. And then something worse happened that I caused. A car wreck. Close they said, neither of us died, but he wanted last rites. We never saw each other again. That's what this is for. To say I'm sorry. I was a boy then, and now an overgrown man, I still remember him when I was a dumb boy and he was my friend.

PUBLICATION CREDITS

The following are the original publication credits for the essays collected in this book. "We Have Been Here All Along" and "Fights" are previously unpublished.

Gilb, Dagoberto. "A Little Bit of Fun before He Died." *Zyzzyva* (Fall 2012). Reprinted in *Best American Essays 2013*. Boston: Houghton Mifflin, 2013.

———. "A Los Cielos de México." *Fresh Air*, National Public Radio, WHYY, Philadelphia, radio essay, December 19, 2017.

———. "A Passing West." Published as "Pride and Prejudice." *Texas Monthly* (February 2013).

———. "Border Petroglyphs." Published as "Raising Hackles on the Border." *Los Angeles Times*, September 6, 2002.

———. "Doors in Old Guate." Published as "Walking Old Guate." *Threepenny Review* (Fall 2018).

———. "Father Close, Father Far." *Threepenny Review* (Summer 2009).

———. "The First Resident of Belken County." *Texas Monthly* (August 2014).

———. "Hecho en Tejas." In *Hecho en Tejas: An Anthology of Texas Mexican Literature*. Albuquerque: University of New Mexico Press, 2006. Reprinted in *Texas Observer*, January 12, 2007.

———. "The Hexagon of the Conquest." *Callaloo* (Spring 2010). *Barcelona Review* (Summer 2010).

———. "How Books Bounce." In "A Study of Dagoberto Gilb: The Author Reflects on Three Stories." *The Bedford Introduction to Literature: Reading, Thinking, Writing*, 10th edition. Boston: Bedford/St. Martin's, 2013.

———. "Huizache." Foreword to *Huizache* no. 9. (Fall 2022).

———. "Hurray for Losers!" *Huizache* no. 7 (Fall 2017). Reprinted in *Tale of Two Americas,* edited by John Freeman. New York: O/R Books, 2017.

———. "Las Milpas en Iowa." Excerpted in *Slate,* September 9, 2008. *Callaloo* (Winter 2009).

———. "La Próxima Parada Is Next." *American Book Review* (April 2011).

———. "Now You Don't See Us, Still You Don't." TEDx talk, 2015, El Paso, TX.

———. "Oily Hair con Slicked Back Notes on Greasy Literature." *Aztlan* (Fall 2007).

———. "Remembering the Alamo." *Los Angeles Times,* April 9, 2004. Syndicated to *San Antonio Express-News, Houston Chronicle,* and *Dallas Morning News.*

———. "Rivera and Rulfo." Published as "Tomás Rivera & Juan Rulfo: Two Stories." In *Reaching Inside: 50 Acclaimed Authors on 100 Unforgettable Stories,* edited by Andre Dubus III. Boston: Godine, 2023.

———. "Snow Angel." *Los Angeles Review of Books,* April 5, 2021.

———. "Texas Lit." In *Texas Literature: A Case Study.* Boston: Bedford/St. Martin's, 2006.

———. "The One Who Left." *Los Angeles Times,* January 14, 2004. *Houston Chronicle,* January 21, 2004. *San Antonio Express-News,* January 25, 2004. Published as "Documentando a los indocumentados," *Contratiempo* (Chicago), February 2004.

———. "Thou Shalt Not Steal Books." In *The Library Book,* Santa Barbara Public Library, 2017. *Los Angeles Review of Books Magazine,* August 2017. Reprinted in *LARB* online edition, September 22, 2017.

———. "Tomato Potatoe, Chalupa Shaloopa." Published as "Taco Bell Nation." *West* (magazine of the *Los Angeles Times*), March 19, 2006. Reprinted in *Mexican-American Cuisine,* edited by Ilan Stavans. Westport, CT: Greenwood Publishing, 2011.